DEADLY DISEASES AND EPIDEMICS

TUBERCULOSIS

SECOND EDITION

DEADLY DISEASES AND EPIDEMICS

DEADLY DISEASES AND EPIDEMICS

TUBERCULOSIS

SECOND EDITION

Kim R. Finer and Alan Hecht, D.C.

Consulting Editor
Hilary Babcock, M.D., M.P.H.,
Infectious Diseases Division,
Washington University School of Medicine,
Medical Director of Occupational Health (Infectious Diseases),
Barnes–Jewish Hospital and St. Louis Children's Hospital

Foreword by
David Heymann
World Health Organization

CHELSEA HOUSE
An Infobase Learning Company

Tuberculosis, Second Edition

Copyright © 2011 by Infobase Learning

Chelsea House
An imprint of Infobase Learning
132 West 31st Street
New York NY 10001

Library of Congress Cataloging-in-Publication Data

Finer, Kim Renee, 1956–
    Tuberculosis / Kim R. Finer and Alan Hecht ; consulting editor, Hilary Babcock ; foreword by David Heymann. — 2nd ed.
        p. cm. — (Deadly diseases and epidemics)
    Includes bibliographical references and index.
    ISBN-13: 978-1-61753-017-3 (hardcover : alk. paper)
    ISBN-10: 1-61753-017-4 (hardcover : alk. paper)   1. Tuberculosis—Juvenile literature. I. Hecht, Alan. II. Title. III. Series.
    RC311.1.F54 2011
    616.9'95—dc22   2011011157

You can find Chelsea House on the World Wide Web at
http://www.infobaselearning.com

Text design by Terry Malon
Cover design by Takeshi Takahashi
Composition by Newgen North America
Cover printed by Yurchak Printing, Landisville, Pa.
Book printed and bound by Yurchak Printing, Landisville, Pa.
Date printed: September 2011
Printed in the United States of America

This book is printed on acid-free paper.

Table of Contents

Foreword

Communicable diseases kill and cause long-term disability. The microbial agents that cause them are dynamic, changeable, and resilient: They are responsible for more than 14 million deaths each year mainly in developing countries.

Approximately 46% of all deaths in the developing world are due to communicable diseases, and almost 90% of these deaths are from AIDS, tuberculosis, malaria, and acute diarrheal and respiratory infections of children. In addition to causing great human suffering these high-mortality communicable diseases have become major obstacles to economic development. They are a challenge to control either because of the lack of effective vaccines, or because the drugs that are used to treat them are becoming less effective because of antimicrobial drug resistance.

Millions of people, especially those who are poor and living in developing countries, are also at risk from disabling communicable diseases such as polio, leprosy, lymphatic filariasis, and onchocerciasis. In addition to human suffering and permanent disability, these communicable diseases create an economic burden—both on the workforce that handicapped persons are unable to join, and on their families and society, upon which they must often depend for economic support.

Finally, the entire world is at risk of the unexpected communicable diseases, those that are called emerging or reemerging infections. Infection is often unpredictable because risk factors for transmission are not understood, or because it often results from organisms that cross the species barrier from animals to humans. The cause is often viral, such as Ebola and Marburg hemorrhagic fevers and severe acute respiratory syndrome (SARS). In addition to causing human suffering and death, these infections place health workers at great risk and are costly to economies. Infections such as Bovine Spongiform Encephalopathy (BSE) and the associated new human variant of Creutzfeldt-Jakob disease (vCJD) in Europe, and avian influenza A (H5N1) in Asia, are reminders of the seriousness of emerging and reemerging infections. In addition, many of these infections have the potential to cause pandemics, which are a constant threat to our economies and public health security.

Science has given us vaccines and anti-infective drugs that have helped keep infectious diseases under control. Nothing demonstrates the effectiveness of vaccines better than the successful eradication of smallpox, the decrease in polio as the eradication program continues, and the decrease in measles when routine immunization programs are supplemented by mass vaccination campaigns.

Likewise, the effectiveness of anti-infective drugs is clearly demonstrated through prolonged life or better health in those infected with viral diseases such as AIDS, parasitic infections such as malaria, and bacterial infections such as tuberculosis and pneumococcal pneumonia.

But current research and development is not filling the pipeline for new anti-infective drugs as rapidly as resistance is developing, nor is vaccine development providing vaccines for some of the most common and lethal communicable diseases. At the same time, providing people with access to existing anti-infective drugs, vaccines, and goods such as condoms or bed nets—necessary for the control of communicable diseases in many developing countries—remains a great challenge.

Education, experimentation, and the discoveries that grow from them are the tools needed to combat high-mortality infectious diseases, diseases that cause disability, or emerging and reemerging infectious diseases. At the same time, partnerships between developing and industrialized countries can overcome many of the challenges of access to goods and technologies. This book may inspire its readers to set out on the path of drug and vaccine development, or on the path to discovering better public health technologies by applying our current understanding of the human genome and those of various infectious agents. Readers may likewise be inspired to help ensure wider access to those protective goods and technologies. Such inspiration, with pragmatic action, will keep us on the winning side of the struggle against communicable diseases.

David L. Heymann
Assistant Director General
Health Security and Environment
Representative of the Director General for Polio Eradication
World Health Organization
Geneva, Switzerland

1

Tuberculosis Throughout Time

On August 3, 1962, Eleanor Roosevelt was admitted to Columbia-Presbyterian Hospital in New York City suffering from a fever of 102 degrees, anemia, and a cough of several weeks' duration. Her doctors immediately suspected tuberculosis. Standard practice dictated that X-rays be taken immediately, but they turned out to be negative for the typical signs of tuberculosis of the lungs. This suggested that no active infection was present.

There were, however, old scars present, which indicated a prior exposure to the disease. This most likely occurred in 1919 when she had a respiratory problem and was told she had pleurisy, a nontubercular infection of the lungs. The infection was probably tuberculosis, but, at the time, her immune system was strong enough to fight it off and the bacteria remained dormant in her lung tissue.

Because Roosevelt had been suffering with anemia prior to her hospital admission, as well as experiencing a reduction in the number of white blood cells and platelets, her doctors administered prednisone, a corticosteroid known to increase the production of all blood cells by stimulating the bone marrow to produce them. Unfortunately, one of prednisone's side effects is partial suppression of the immune system, which makes an individual more susceptible to infections and diseases.

Her doctors, knowing that her immune system was suppressed and that she most likely had tuberculosis in the past, began treating her with isoniazid and streptomycin, two modern antibiotics that worked particularly well against tuberculosis. Despite this, her condition continued to worsen, and on October 12 her fever reached 105 degrees. Her family agreed with her request to her doctors upon her admission that she not die in the hospital, so *she was discharged on October 18. The doctors could not make a definitive diagnosis. They did, however, take a bone marrow sample to culture for Mycobacterium tuberculosis before she left the hospital. On October 26, the culture grew the tuberculosis bacteria, which suggested that an old and previously contained infection had come back from dormancy thanks to the prednisone treatment. On November 4, 1962, Eleanor Roosevelt had a stroke that left her in a coma. She died on November 7.*

An autopsy performed the next day proved that she had miliary tuberculosis. The bacteria had spread throughout her body from the original site in the lungs and had invaded her lungs, liver, kidneys, and brain. The question arose as to why the medications didn't work to cure her. The strain of Mycobacterium tuberculosis she was infected with was resistant to both medications. Since she was diligent about taking her medications this seemed impossible. As it turned out, she was most likely exposed to an individual who had a resistant strain of the bacteria and became easily infected because her immune system was being suppressed by the prednisone. So, although possible, it was most likely not a dormant tuberculosis infection that eventually killed her.[1]

Fredric Chopin, Edgar Allan Poe, Eleanor Roosevelt, Charlotte Brontë, John Keats, Henry David Thoreau, King Edward IV, Doc Holliday—the list of the rich, famous, and infamous who became victims of tuberculosis is long and recognizable. Writers, politicians, scientists, poets—all segments of society were affected. Even today tuberculosis remains a public health threat. Nearly one-third of the world's population is currently infected, and approximately 9.4 million people became newly infected in 2009. Approximately 1.7 million people died from the disease in 2008.

Tuberculosis was first described in ancient times. Scientists believe that the disease established itself firmly in human populations about the time humans transitioned from nomadic tribes to settled, agriculturally based societies (8000 B.C.). These

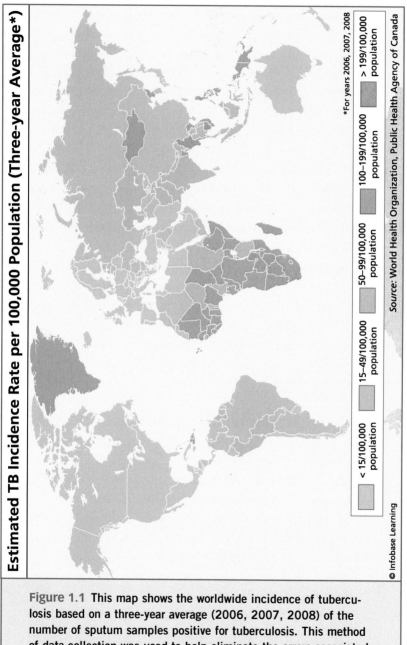

Estimated TB Incidence Rate per 100,000 Population (Three-year Average*)

*For years 2006, 2007, 2008

> 199/100,000 population

100–199/100,000 population

50–99/100,000 population

15–49/100,000 population

< 15/100,000 population

Source: World Health Organization, Public Health Agency of Canada

© Infobase Learning

Figure 1.1 This map shows the worldwide incidence of tuberculosis based on a three-year average (2006, 2007, 2008) of the number of sputum samples positive for tuberculosis. This method of data collection was used to help eliminate the errors associated with relying only on reported cases as there are most likely many unreported cases.

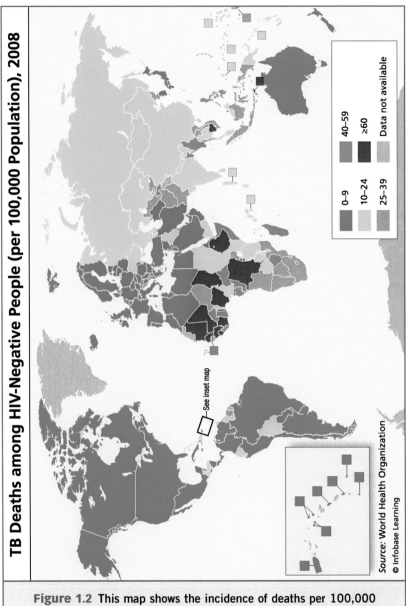

Figure 1.2 This map shows the incidence of deaths per 100,000 people worldwide in 2008 due to tuberculosis. Note that the highest rates are found in the poorest countries.

settlements provided sufficiently large groups through which the disease-causing microbes could find susceptible hosts.

EVIDENCE OF TUBERCULOSIS IN EGYPT

The earliest archeological evidence of tuberculosis comes from ancient Egypt. Bones of Egyptian mummies dating from 2400 B.C. show evidence of decay caused by *Mycobacterium tuberculosis*, the bacterium that causes the disease tuberculosis. Many of these remains show erosion and fusion of the vertebrae, a result of infection by the organism. Tubercle bacilli have also been identified in bones dated to the period. The spinal form of tuberculosis, called **Pott's disease**, appears to have been particularly common in ancient Egypt. Depictions of hunchbacked slaves as well as nobles are recognized in Egyptian art as far back as 3000 B.C.

Descriptions of typical signs and symptoms associated with tuberculosis, which include the coughing of blood, fevers, night sweats, and weight loss or wasting, can be found in ancient writings. Clearly, people of the time recognized this malady as an evil for which neither priests nor gods could offer a cure.

GREEK AND ROMAN INTEREST IN TUBERCULOSIS

The ancient Greeks had a genuine interest in medicine, which they considered a science rather than being in the realm of religion, as many cultures believed. Greek scholars wrote on many medical subjects, including tuberculosis. The Greeks called tuberculosis "**phthisis**." Although a clear derivation and definition of the word is not generally agreed upon, it may come from the ancient Greek word that means "to waste" or "consume." **Consumption** is the term used in the Old Testament of the Bible to describe tuberculosis, and both terms, phthisis and consumption, were used by the Greeks, Romans, Hebrews, and eventually Europeans, to describe tuberculosis through the early 1900s.

The Greek physician Hippocrates mentioned tuberculosis in many of his writings and is believed to have first used the word *phthisis* to describe the disease. Hippocrates speculated that the disease was caused by growths that he observed in the lungs. His writings also suggest that he associated tuberculosis of the spine with the same disease occurring in the lungs.

Although best known as a Greek philosopher, Plato was also trained as a physician. Plato provided a practical, if not ethical, warning against the treatment of tuberculosis. He advised that treating patients with the disease "was of no advantage to themselves or to the State" because the patients would most likely die.

Around A.D. 162, the Greek physician **Galen**, a favorite of the Roman emperor Marcus Aurelius, practiced medicine in Rome. Galen, an astute observer who performed necropsies on animals and wrote anatomy texts, guessed that tuberculosis might be infectious. He prescribed a treatment for the disease consisting of fresh milk, open air, sea breezes, and dry, mountainous places. Because the infectious nature of the disease remained a mystery, this prescription would be the best that medicine had to offer for the treatment of tuberculosis for almost the next 1,700 years!

THE MIDDLE AGES

The years that followed the great Roman Empire included very little writing about, or interest in, science or medicine. Religious thought dominated this period, known as the Dark Ages, and religious zealots discouraged inquiry or scientific explanation of natural events. Consequently, little is known of the extent or incidence of tuberculosis during this time. The one form of tuberculosis we do know about during medieval times was an infliction known as **scrofula**. Scrofula is the name given to tuberculosis of the lymph nodes. When infected, these nodes (knotlike masses of tissue) become enlarged and rubbery to the touch. Early monarchs, who believed they ruled through divine power, claimed the power to heal scrofula by touch. King Edward I of England (reigned 1272–1307) is said to have touched 533 afflicted subjects in a single month in 1277, and in the 1600s, King Henry VII began the practice of giving a gold angel or amulet to those he touched. Shakespeare, the great English playwright, described this ritual to cure scrofula in his play *Macbeth*.

Figure 1.3 Although originally from Greece, Claude Galen, pictured above, practiced medicine in Rome. He had a keen interest in the workings of the human body. In addition to his research in tuberculosis, he spent a great deal of his professional life studying the circulatory system. (National Library of Medicine)

'Tis called the Evil:
A most miraculous work in this good king;
Which often since my here-remain in England
I have seen him do. How he solicits heaven,
Himself best knows; but strangely visited people,
All swoln and ulcerous, pitiful to the eye,
The mere despair of surgery, he cures;
Hanging a golden stamp about their necks,
Put on with holy prayers; and 'tis spoken,
To the succeeding royalty he leaves
The healing benediction.

—Macbeth, IV, iii, 146

As Europe emerged from the Dark Ages, there was a renaissance not only of art but also medicine and science. This interest in science coincided with the tuberculosis epidemic in Europe that began in the early 1600s and continued over the next two centuries. Increased population centers, as well as poverty, contributed to the growing number of cases. Tuberculosis became known as the Great White Plague because it caused the complexions of its victims to become very pale, and was almost as feared as the Black Death or bubonic plague of earlier times.

TUBERCULOSIS IN THE AMERICAS

Some historians have suggested that along with a few other plagues, Columbus brought tuberculosis to the new world. However, in 1994 scientists from Minnesota dispelled that theory. They used sophisticated molecular techniques and discovered DNA from *Mycobacterium tuberculosis* in the fossilized remains of a woman in her forties who lived with, but apparently did not die from, tuberculosis. This woman lived in an arid desert region of Peru almost 400 years before Columbus discovered America. From this evidence one can conclude that tuberculosis was present in the Americas before Columbus ever set foot in the region.

Although we have evidence that tuberculosis was present in the Americas prior to the arrival of European settlers, Native Americans of North and South America had little trouble with tuberculosis, in part due to the fact that there were few major population centers. Tuberculosis organisms that lack a large number of susceptible hosts living close together fail to establish disease in a population.

Tuberculosis remained a rare disease among native North Americans well into the 1800s, and would only become a problem when these indigenous people were forced into reservations, barracks, or prison camps. In these settings, contacts with European Americans became more frequent, and the crowding promoted airborne transmission of the bacterium. In 1886, the death rate for Native Americans from tuberculosis was 90 per 1000 individuals, a figure 10 times greater than the highest death rate in Europe in the 1600s!

THE DISEASE ROMANTICIZED

Tuberculosis was feared throughout the 1600s, but it was romanticized during the 1700s, 1800s, and early 1900s. The gaunt, fragile, vulnerable look of consumption became fashionable. It was considered glamorous to look sickly. Camille Saint-Säens, a famous composer, wrote in 1913 that "it was fashionable to be pale and drained." The dying young person was often thought to possess a romantic personality and have creative gifts. This was especially true among those in literature and the arts. The poet Percy Shelley wrote to fellow poet John Keats, "This consumption is a disease particularly fond of people who write such good verses as you have done." John Keats, who studied medicine and was torn between writing poetry and practicing medicine, was very familiar with tuberculosis. His mother died of the disease when Keats was 14 years old, and his brother later developed tuberculosis. In the summer of 1829, Keats noticed blood when he coughed deeply. He immediately recognized this sign as a death warrant and was dead one year later.

DID YOU KNOW?

The literary Brontë family was hit particularly hard by tuberculosis. The Reverend Patrick Brontë and his wife Marie had six children. Marie died at age 38 shortly after the birth of her last child from childbed fever, a condition of the 1800s that resulted in the death of a significant number of women who had recently given birth (although she may also have had tuberculosis). Reverend Brontë had a chronic cough that was probably caused by tuberculosis. Maria, the oldest Brontë daughter, died from tuberculosis at age 12, and her sister Elizabeth died one month later at age 11. Two years later, Branwell, the Brontës' only son, died at age 25, with sister Emily (author of *Wuthering Heights*) dying a few months later at the age of 30. Anne died at age 29, five months after Emily, and Charlotte (author of *Jane Eyre*) died from tuberculosis at age 39. Amazingly, Reverend Brontë lived until the age of 85.

Robert Louis Stevenson, another famous writer of the time (*Treasure Island, Dr. Jekyll and Mr. Hyde, Kidnapped*), developed tuberculosis as a child, but the course of his disease contrasted greatly with that of Keats. Beginning at the age of 25, Stevenson traveled around the world trying to find a climate where he would be free of his tuberculosis symptoms. After spending time in France and Switzerland, he eventually became a patient at **Edward Trudeau's sanatorium** in Saranac Lake, New York. Although Stevenson had tuberculosis throughout his adult life, he was not overly weakened by the disease. He continued to travel and write until he died at the age of 44 of a condition unrelated to his tuberculosis.

In the 1700s, many causes were attributed to tuberculosis: heredity (the Brontë family provided excellent evidence for this theory), unfavorable climate, laziness, depression, and lack of air and light. The most famous pathologist of the late 1800s, Rudolf Virchow, refused to believe tuberculosis was infectious. However, other scientists did not share this view. Those scientists were carrying out experiments and making observations that would eventually reveal the cause of the disease.

THE TRUE NATURE OF THE DISEASE

In the early 1700s an English physician named Benjamin Marten wrote a book entitled *A New Theory of Consumption: More Especially of a Phthisis or Consumption of the Lungs*. In his book, Dr. Marten suggested that tuberculosis might be caused by the "wonderfully minute living creatures," or the animalcules described by Anton von Leeuwenhoek, inventor of a microscope able to view bacteria and fungi in 1676. Marten wrote his book 160 years before the bacterium was viewed and described by the German physician **Robert Koch**, and shown to be connected to disease. Unfortunately, the book went unnoticed by most scientists of Dr. Marten's day.

It was not until 1865 that a formal demonstration proving that tuberculosis could be transmitted was conducted. Jean-Antoine Villemin, a French physician, inoculated rabbits with pus and fluid from human and cattle tuberculosis lesions. When he examined the lungs and lymph nodes of the dead rabbits he found tubercular lesions.

With the above descriptions and discoveries, the stage was set for learning the true cause of tuberculosis. Although the discipline of microbiology was in its infancy, the burgeoning interest in the study of microorganisms was about to provide information about the causes and even cures for many of the deadly diseases that had been plaguing humans since ancient times.

2

Robert Koch, Selman Waksman, and the Near Defeat of Tuberculosis

John began feeling ill. He was running a fever, had a persistent cough with chest pains, felt very run down, and just wanted to stay in bed. His family urged him to see a doctor even if he did just have the flu as so many of his friends and even he himself believed.

It was early 1947, and John felt that, since there was no treatment for the flu, a visit to the doctor was a waste of time and effort. But he wanted his family to stop nagging him, so he went.

The doctor examined him thoroughly and immediately sent him for a chest X-ray. The results were not encouraging. John had small opaque lesions in several places in both lungs. Based on the symptoms and X-ray findings, the diagnosis was pulmonary tuberculosis.

The doctor was not disheartened, however, as he had recently read of a clinical trial testing a new antibiotic called **streptomycin** *that seemed to have great success at treating tuberculosis. The drug was now available on the market, so he prescribed it for John to use. Within several months, John was on the road to being cured.*

Robert Koch was born December 11, 1843, one of 13 children in Clausthal, Lower Saxony, Germany. As a young boy he had an interest in nature and spent much of his time collecting plants and insects. At the age of 19, Koch entered the University at Göttingen, Germany, where he was an outstanding student (although he was not a particularly good student before entering the university). While at the university, he won a research prize and published two scientific papers. He received his doctorate at the age of 23 and began practicing medicine at the Hamburg General Hospital. He later married his childhood sweetheart and went into private medical practice.

When war broke out between Germany and France in 1870, Koch tried to enlist in the army but was rejected because of his poor eyesight. Upon his second attempt at enlisting, he was accepted to serve as a doctor. Koch served in a battlefield hospital where his war experience affected him greatly. He became very nationalistic, and violently anti-French (this would affect him later in his dealings with Louis Pasteur, the famous French microbiologist).

Following the war, Koch went back to his medical practice and also spent time conducting research in his laboratory. He was especially interested in the disease anthrax, which is caused by the bacterium *Bacillus anthracis*. In his laboratory, he was able to culture the anthrax bacillus in liquid media and view the organism using the microscope his wife had purchased for him as a birthday present. Koch was also able to observe the development of spores from the anthrax bacilli, thereby linking the bacillus to the spores found in the blood of anthrax-infected animals. Koch presented his research in April 1876 to a group from the Institute of Plant Science in Breslau. The audience of scientists was very impressed; Koch had clearly established that bacteria cause the disease anthrax.

Ferdinand Cohn, director of the Institute of Plant Science, was so impressed with Koch's research that he was able to secure a position for the young scientist at the Imperial Health Office in Berlin. During his first year in Berlin, Koch was a very busy man; he developed the steam method of sterilization, he showed that the bacteria streptococci and staphylococci could cause wound infections, he was the first scientist to use an oil immersion lens to view bacteria, and he developed a solid culture medium on which to grow pure cultures of bacteria.

Koch began his work on tuberculosis in 1881. He was assisted in the laboratory by Freidrich Loeffler and Georg Gaffky. Both men would later go on to make famous discoveries

Figure 2.1 Koch is one of the founders of the discipline of microbiology. He studied anthrax, cholera, and tuberculosis, and attempted to create a tuberculosis vaccine. Koch also developed a set of rules for all scientists to follow to identify microorganisms that produced specific diseases. Known as Koch's postulates, they are still a fundamental aspect of microbiology. Koch is pictured here at the age of 62, as he appeared in 1905 in his Nobel Prize photograph. (© The Nobel Foundation)

themselves. After only seven months of work, Koch presented his research on tuberculosis at the monthly meeting of the Berlin Physiological Society. At that meeting, Koch presented proof that *Mycobacterium tuberculosis* (*Bacillus tuberculosis* was the name used by Koch) was the cause of the disease tuberculosis. In his presentation, Koch put forth the steps he used while working with anthrax bacilli to arrive at his conclusions. These steps, known as **Koch's postulates**, are still used today to establish that a particular bacterium causes a specific disease.

Although Koch turned his attention for a brief time to cholera, he continued to search for a cure for tuberculosis. Robert Koch was a great scientist, but his personal pride, a tendency toward not sharing experimental results with other scientists, and perhaps a sense of German nationalism caused an unfortunate blunder regarding the development of a tuberculosis vaccine.

Under great pressure from the German government to prove its country's intellectual superiority, Koch publicly stated in 1890 that he had developed a method for producing resistance against the tuberculosis bacterium, a vaccine called **tuberculin**. In the words of Koch he had "found substances that halted the growth of tuberculosis bacilli not only in test tubes but also in animal bodies."[1] Unfortunately, the vaccine, which

MAKING THEIR OWN MARK

Koch's first two assistants, Fredrich Loeffler and Georg Gaffky, went on to become famous for their own discoveries. Loeffler discovered the cause of diphtheria, and Gaffky described the cause of cholera. The Gaffky scale is used today to describe the number of tubercle bacilli in the sputum of tuberculosis patients. The scale ranges from 1 (with 1–4 organisms per microscopic field) to 9 (with an average of 100 organisms per field).

KOCH'S POSTULATES

Although technology has increased the speed at which we can detect or diagnose disease, some things have not changed. Today, 130 years after Koch first described them, the set of steps known as Koch's postulates are still used to determine that a particular organism causes a particular disease. The steps are as follows:

1. Isolation of the bacterium from sick and dying animals.
2. Growth and identification of the organism in the laboratory.
3. Reproduction of the disease in a previously healthy laboratory animal by inoculation with the organism.
4. Isolation of the organisms from the laboratory animal in which the disease was reproduced and careful comparison to determine a "match" with the original disease-causing bacterium.

had been tested only in guinea pigs, produced serious and sometimes deadly side effects in humans. When data ultimately showed the vaccine to be ineffective, Koch's reputation was somewhat tarnished. Nonetheless, Koch still was awarded the Nobel Prize in medicine in 1905 for his studies on tuberculosis.

Following Koch's retirement as the director of the Institute for Infectious Disease in Berlin, Koch and his wife traveled extensively. Robert Koch died in 1910 at the age of 66 from a heart attack.

THE MAGIC BULLET

While the most widely prescribed treatment for tuberculosis, even after Koch's discovery, remained the advice of Galen (rest, sea travel, and fresh air), governments and the public began to mobilize their efforts to defeat the disease. In 1892, the first local tuberculosis association was formed in Philadelphia. The

Christmas Seal program, initially sponsored by the Red Cross and taken over by the National Tuberculosis Association in 1920, began to raise a great deal of money to fund tuberculosis research. X-rays, discovered in 1895 by William Roentgen, were being used to rapidly screen millions of Americans for lung lesions, while local regulations against spitting and/or coughing in public were enforced. The **BCG vaccine** against tuberculosis was being used in Europe, although its effectiveness was a point of debate.

With the knowledge that bacteria were responsible for causing tuberculosis, campaigns were started to try to stop the spread of the disease, especially before actual antibiotic treatments were developed. The medical community realized that prevention was an effective way of reducing the number of disease cases when an actual treatment wasn't yet available.

In 1904, the National Association for the Study and Prevention of Tuberculosis was created to help educate the public on ways to prevent the spread of tuberculosis and expand regional tuberculosis programs. Its work included an aggressive campaign against public spitting. During the next several years, other associations were created throughout the United States, all with the same purpose. The Rensselaer County Tuberculosis Association in Troy, New York, was one of these groups that also campaigned for methods to halt the spread of tuberculosis.

Selman Waksman was born in 1888 in Odessa, Ukraine. As a young man he moved to the United States and attended Rutgers University, in New Jersey, where he studied a group of soil bacteria called actinomycetes. He eventually earned his Ph.D. and became a recognized expert in the field of soil microbiology. With the advent of World War II, Waksman decided to pursue research in the area of **antibiotics**, substances produced by one microorganism that can inhibit the growth of, or kill, other microorganisms. Waksman's interest in antibiotics combined with his knowledge of actinomycetes culminated in

Figure 2.2 Selman Waksman, pictured here, first discovered the use of streptomycin as an antibiotic. Streptomycin was tested in a woman who was suffering from tuberculosis in 1944. Although the antibiotic was not a perfect solution, as it had some side effects and did not always cure the disease, it gave hope to tuberculosis patients and paved the way for future research. (Waksman Foundation for Microbiology)

the isolation of the antibiotic streptomycin, a product of the soil actinomycete, *Streptomyces griseus* in 1943.

Streptomycin was first used in humans in 1944 to treat a young woman dying of tuberculosis. At first, a crude preparation was used to treat her disease, and she failed to improve. In early 1945, a more purified form of the antibiotic became available for use. The new preparation was administered to the woman described above. She immediately began to get better. The number of tubercle bacilli in her sputum decreased and one of her lungs showed marked improvement. A follow-up exam of the patient 10 years later showed that the disease had remained inactive as a result of the streptomycin treatment.

Initial hopes for streptomycin were somewhat dashed because the antibiotic produced side effects in some patients and did not destroy the organism in others. Even worse, in some patients, antibiotic-resistant forms of the tubercle bacilli began to emerge. Fortunately, more effective antibiotics with fewer side effects would soon become available, including para-aminosalicylic acid in 1948, isoniazid in 1951, ethambutol in 1961, and rifampin in 1967.

With the use of antibiotics to treat tuberculosis, Galen's prescription was finally replaced. As a consequence, sanatoriums that had been established to treat tuberculosis sufferers began to close. The impact of public health programs and treating the disease with antibiotics produced a constant decline in the number of tuberculosis cases from 1959 until the mid-1980s. Yet tuberculosis is still with us. The disease continues to present new public health challenges by targeting particular segments of the population and "teaming" with **AIDS (acquired immune deficiency syndrome).**

3

The Tuberculosis Bacterium

Helga was a physician in the late 1800s in Germany. She was often exposed to many different diseases as she treated her patients and frequently considered herself lucky that she didn't catch any of them. As much as she didn't want to think about it, the fear that one day her luck would run out was always in the back of her mind.

One morning, Helga woke up feeling somewhat ill. She noticed that a cough was beginning to develop and figured it was just a cold she had contracted from a patient she saw a few days ago. She dismissed it and went about her business. Unfortunately, the cough and body aches didn't disappear in a week as she expected they would. Over time the cough got worse, she developed night sweats, she lost weight, was very tired, and tended to run fevers. As a physician, she knew what was developing even though she didn't want to admit it to herself.

*In her mind she wondered what she would do, as there was no medicine to cure the tuberculosis she was almost sure she had. Helga knew that the first thing she needed to do was to make a definitive diagnosis. The question was just how to do this. Then she remembered reading an article in a medical journal about a new stain technique that had been developed by Dr. Paul Ehrlich and improved by Dr. Franz Ziehl and Dr. Friedrich Neelsen. Originally called an **acid-fast stain**, it was now referred to as the Ziehl-Neelsen stain. It was specially designed to stain **Mycobacterium tuberculosis**, which normally didn't stain well with existing techniques.*

Helga collected a sputum sample brought up by one of the many coughs she was experiencing and smeared it on a glass microscope slide. She proceeded to stain it according to the procedure outlined in the journal article. Sadly, when she looked under the microscope, her worst fears were confirmed. She saw the typical rod-shaped, acid-fast bacteria known as Mycobacterium tuberculosis.

Now she pondered what to do to try to beat the disease. Without treatment, her only possibility would be to travel to a warm climate, get a great deal of rest, and eat healthy food. Her next step was to makes plans for a long vacation in a foreign land.

The disease tuberculosis can be caused by one of four different organisms belonging to the genus *Mycobacterium*. **Mycobacterium bovis**, *Mycobacterium africanum, Mycobacterium microti, and Mycobacterium tuberculosis* are the four species that make up the tuberculosis complex. Of the four different organisms, *Mycobacterium tuberculosis* is the most common cause of tuberculosis in human beings. *Mycobacterium africanum* is usually found only in northwestern Africa, and *Mycobacterium bovis*, which causes disease in cattle, is now only a rare cause of human tuberculosis because it is usually destroyed during pasteurization of milk from cattle. All four organisms mentioned are very similar and almost indistinguishable in the laboratory. Only very minor biochemical and genetic differences separate members of the group.

PHYSICAL CHARACTERISTICS

The organism *Mycobacterium tuberculosis* is a slow-growing, long, slender, rod-shaped bacterium. The size of the bacillus falls within the range of 0.2–0.6μm x 1.0–10 μm (a μm equals one-millionth of a meter). In body tissues, the organisms often form long-massed filaments of cells that are called **cords**. The capacity to form cords is related to the organism's **virulence**, or ability of the organism to cause disease.

Like all prokaryotic organisms, the tubercle bacillus is a simple cell. The bacterium is rod-shaped and surrounded by a multilayered cell wall containing mycolic acids. On the inside of the cell wall lies the cell membrane, a lipid bilayer that controls what goes into and out of the bacterium. Lipids are a broad group of organic compounds that do not generally dissolve in water. The best known lipids are fats. On the inside of the cell membrane is the cytoplasm, which contains genetic material, ribosomes, vacuoles, and granules.

Tubercle bacilli do not form capsules, produce flagella, or form spores. They do not produce toxins or many of the other enzymes that are normally associated with the disease process. Although the tuberculosis bacterium has few, if any, of the virulence factors we normally associate with the ability to cause disease, it can still wreak havoc in a susceptible host.

The organism creates problems for the host, in part, because of the makeup of the cell wall. The organism has a cell wall that contains not only the complex carbohydrate **peptidoglycan**, as do other bacteria, but it also contains large waxlike lipids called **mycolic acids**. The mycolic acids of mycobacteria are very large organic molecules containing anywhere from 60 to 90 carbons.

These lipids provide a layer that protects the organism from harsh chemicals, many antibiotics, and antibodies (protective proteins produced by the human host). The mycolic acid of the cell wall also aids in preventing digestion of the organisms by phagocytic cells. The ability to resist being digested allows the organisms to ultimately establish infection and cause disease.

Mycolic acids also make the bacteria resistant to drying. This allows the organism to survive for a long time in dried sputum. This characteristic of the organism poses an infection risk for the unsuspecting victim.

STAINING CHARACTERISTICS OF MYCOBACTERIA

A very important tool in the classification of bacteria is the Gram's stain. This staining method, discovered by Hans Christian Gram in 1884, separates most bacteria into one of two groups: Gram-negative bacteria or Gram-positive bacteria. Gram-positive bacteria have a cell wall composed of a thick layer of peptidoglycan.

Gram-negative bacteria have cell walls composed of a thin layer of peptidoglycan and an additional layer called the outer membrane. When the Gram's stain is performed on mycobacteria, the primary stain will not wash out because of the mycolic acids present. Generally, organisms are considered Gram-positive if they retain the initial stain and color purple, and Gram-negative if the initial stain washes out and the cell takes up the counterstain instead (usually safranin, which gives the bacteria a reddish-pink color). However, this stain does not work on mycobacteria due to the high lipid content of its cell wall.

Since the Gram's stain will not work correctly on the mycobacteria, another stain, the acid-fast stain, is used to differentiate and visualize the organism. In the acid-fast stain, the

DID YOU KNOW?

Hans Christian Joachim Gram was a Danish physician working in the morgue of a Berlin hospital in 1884 when he developed a method to stain bacteria found in infected lung tissue. This staining procedure, now known as the Gram's stain, generally divides the world of bacteria into two groups: Gram-positive bacteria and Gram-negative bacteria. Following completion of the staining procedure, Gram-positive organisms will appear purple and Gram-negative organisms appear pink (or red). This staining distinction is based upon the fact that the two groups of bacteria have cell walls that are structurally and chemically different. Because of their mycolic acid layer, mycobacteria do not stain appropriately with the Gram's stain; therefore, Paul Ehrlich, a pupil of Robert Koch's, developed another stain to differentiate these organisms from others: the acid-fast stain. In this stain, the fuchsia-colored primary stain will not wash out even when using an acid-alcohol—thus the name "acid-fast." Organisms that are not acid-fast will appear blue, which is the color of the counterstain.

primary dye will be retained only if the cell wall of the organism contains mycolic acids.

CHARACTERISTICS OF MYCOBACTERIA IN CULTURE

Mycobacterium tuberculosis grows very slowly. One bacillus takes approximately 20 hours to divide, as opposed to *Escherichia coli*, for example, which replicates approximately every 20 minutes. A colony of *Mycobacteria tuberculosis* will take several weeks to grow large enough to be seen on laboratory media. Some scientists suggest that the slow growth rate is due to the sluggish action of the organism's RNA polymerase, the enzyme responsible for transcribing DNA into RNA, which will ultimately be translated into protein.

When grown in broth cultures, masses of bacilli form in a chainlike fashion on the surface of the media, giving the appearance of dense moldlike layers. The genus name, *Mycobacterium*, is derived from the Greek word *mykes,* which means fungal or mold-like.

It can be difficult to grow mycobacteria in the laboratory because the organisms will not grow on ordinary culture media. Special media containing egg yolk is often used to cultivate the bacilli. When grown at 35°–37°C on solid media, the organism will produce colonies in three to six weeks. These colonies are usually a buff or beige color and have a rough, dry, granular appearance.

Most mycobacteria are strict aerobic organisms, meaning that they require oxygen to grow and reproduce. The oxygen requirement explains why the bacilli reproduce particularly well in the lungs.

GENETICS OF THE ORGANISM

In 1996, the Institute for Genomic Research (abbreviated TIGR, and located in Rockville, Maryland) began sequencing the

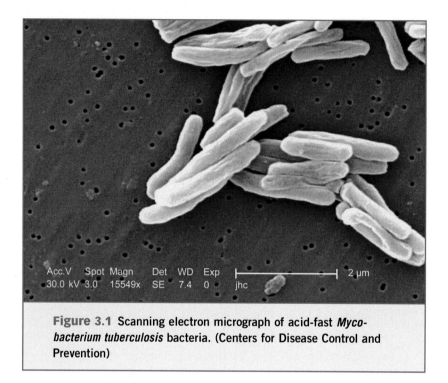

Figure 3.1 Scanning electron micrograph of acid-fast *Mycobacterium tuberculosis* bacteria. (Centers for Disease Control and Prevention)

genome of a strain of *Mycobacterium tuberculosis* called "Oshkosh" or CDC-1551. The Oshkosh strain was originally isolated from a man who worked in a children's clothing factory. The strain was particularly contagious. Approximately 80 percent of the man's coworkers and social contacts were infected by this single individual.

Results from TIGR's sequencing efforts, as well as research at the Sanger Centre in England, indicate that the circular genome of *Mycobacterium tuberculosis* is composed of 4,403,765 base pairs. These bases encode approximately 4,000 genes. Of those genes, 43 percent have known biological roles, 15 percent match genes from other species, and 42 percent have no current database match and probably represent unique genes.

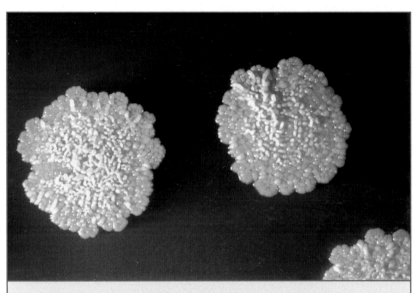

Figure 3.2 *Mycobacterium tuberculosis* colonies grow very slowly, and can be cultivated only on special media. Cultures grown in broth have a funguslike appearance. Cultures grown on solid media, shown here, have a beige-colored, dry, granular appearance. The tuberculosis bacteria require oxygen to grow and reproduce, which is one reason why the bacteria favor the lungs. (Center for Tuberculosis Research, Johns Hopkins University)

Table 3.1 **Target Genes for Tuberculosis Therapy and Their Functions**

Gene Name	Function
icl	Gene that codes for an enzyme that makes fatty acids available for energy
erp	Gene that codes for an enzyme that makes fatty acids available for energy
pcaA	Gene that plays a role in the strength of the cell wall and ability to form cords
sigF	Regulatory gene that controls survival in tubercles

Scientists are looking to these unique genes and their proteins as well as other genes for clues as to how the organism persists in the body and successfully outwits the host's immune system. Several genes are now being investigated as potential drug or vaccine targets. Of particular interest are those genes that enable the organism to survive inside the macrophage. These include genes for lipid metabolism, cell wall synthesis, and regulation of transcription.

4

Consumption: What Happens Once You Become Infected

On a flight from Paris to New York in 1998, more than 250 passengers inhaled and exhaled the same cabin air not knowing that one of them had a severe cough. During the course of the next few months, 12 individuals on the flight were diagnosed with tuberculosis. Were the victims infected by one individual during an eight-hour flight? What about the other 237 passengers and flight crew? Why didn't they become infected? Maybe some of them did — and they just didn't realize it.

TUBERCULOSIS INFECTION

It may take as few as eight to ten tuberculosis bacilli to cause tuberculosis infection. Upon inhalation, the organisms contained in **droplet nuclei** (small droplets of sputum containing two to three bacilli) enter the body and make their way deep into the lungs where they will be ingested by special phagocytic cells called **macrophages**. Macrophages are responsible for acting as sentinels to keep unwanted organisms out of the lower respiratory tract.

Following macrophage ingestion, the war between host and microorganism begins. The situation can have two possible outcomes depending upon the killing power of the host's macrophages and the ability of the organism to cause disease. Strong phagocytic cells may ingest and destroy the bacilli, preventing both infection and disease. Alternately, the invading

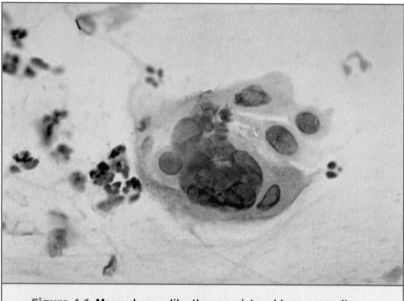

Figure 4.1 Macrophages, like the one pictured here, are cells of the body's defense system. They act as soldiers to protect the body and attack foreign invaders. Macrophages are a type of phagocytic cell. Phagocyte means "eating cell" and these cells literally swallow the invading microorganism whole. (© Lester V. Bergman/Corbis)

organisms may continue to live and even replicate inside the phagocytic cell. While inside the phagocytic cells, many organisms are carried to the lymph nodes. Lymph nodes are small structures found throughout the body that filter out harmful substances and act as collection sites for **lymphocytes**. In the lymph nodes, the organisms may be destroyed or continue to grow and eventually **lyse**, or break open, the host phagocytic cells, thus gaining access to other parts of the body.

If the bacilli remain alive in the host's cells, one to four weeks after the initial infection the host's specific immune system will begin to mount an organized attack against the tuberculosis bacilli. Macrophages seek out and organize around the

DID YOU KNOW?

There are many different types of cells that function in the immune response. Phagocytic cells, or "cells that eat," are immune cells responsible for ingesting and destroying anything the body perceives as "non-self." Phagocytic cells come in one of two types: those that have granules in their cytoplasm (granulocytes) and those that do not (agranulocytes). A macrophage is a type of agranulocyte that is found in the tissues and is highly efficient at eliminating foreign materials from the body. Although macrophages are found in all tissues, they are present in large numbers in the lungs, liver, spleen, and lymph nodes. Lymphocytes are another group of immune cells. Lymphocytes (B cells and T cells) have no phagocytic capability, but play major roles in the specific immune response. B cells produce antibodies and T cells directly kill or release compounds that ultimately lead to the death of the invading microorganisms.

bacteria, forming large-multinucleated cells called "**giant cells**." Additional macrophages and other immune cells called lymphocytes begin to assemble and wall off the bacteria. The collection of immune cells, bacilli, and host cells forms a **tubercle** (from the Latin word for knob or swelling).

These tubercles wall off and may hold the organism in check throughout the rest of the infected person's life. In some infected individuals, the tubercle may decay due to the release of enzymes by the bacteria and host cells. This decay results in soft, cheesy ooze, called **caseous exudate**, in the center of the lesion. This lesion may become calcified and heal—again halting the infection and containing the organisms. The calcified tubercles are sometimes visible on an X-ray of an infected person's chest.

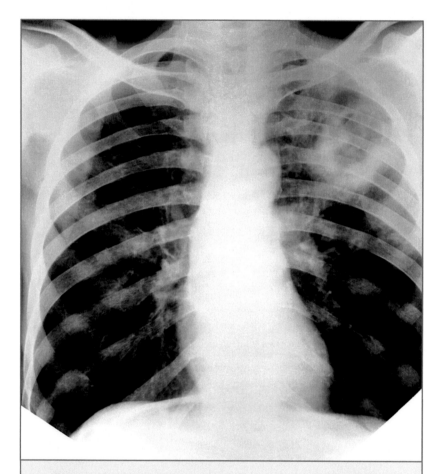

Figure 4.2 Tubercules can effectively contain the bacillus, or they can decay into an oozy lesion. These lesions can calcify and form deposits within the lungs, containing the infection once more. These calcifications can be seen in an X-ray. The chest X ray pictured here shows tubercle calcifications in the upper left area of the lung (upper right portion of the X-ray). These spots represent formerly active foci of *Mycobacterium tuberculosis* infection. (© Lester V. Bergman/Corbis)

The entire story might end at this stage with no further complications. People who have the tuberculosis *infection* just described do not feel sick, have no symptoms, and are not infectious. They have what is known as **latent tuberculosis**. Individuals with latent tuberculosis will have a positive result from a tuberculosis test and can develop tuberculosis later in life (reactivation) if their immune system becomes weak.

TUBERCULOSIS DISEASE

If the tubercle ruptures and releases organisms into either the bloodstream or the bronchi, infected material may spread throughout the body or further into the lungs. When the organism spreads throughout the body, it can produce small yellow nodules one to two millimeters in diameter. This form of disseminated tuberculosis is often called **miliary tuberculosis** because the nodules resemble the grain millet.

The mechanism by which tuberculosis bacilli spread is an interesting one. The bacteria erode a pulmonary vein and enter the blood that is returning to the heart. As they travel through the blood, they eventually enter the left ventricle of the heart, which pumps blood to the systemic circulation. The bacteria are now able to access any organ in the body.

Another route that the bacilli may take is to enter a lymphatic vessel in the lungs. These vessels eventually empty into the venous blood circulation, bringing the bacteria to the right side of the heart. The right ventricle pumps blood to the lungs for oxygenation, so the bacteria are able to enter the lung tissue again to bring about further infection of the tissue.[1]

The unchecked replication and dissemination of tuberculosis bacilli is indicative of tuberculosis *disease*. Tuberculosis disease occurs in about 10% of individuals who have the tuberculosis infection. Tuberculosis disease is usually the result of a weakened immune system that can no longer contain the invading organisms.

Physical signs that someone has the disease include: a severe cough that may include bloody sputum (called **hemoptysis**), loss of appetite, weight loss, weakness, chills, night sweats, and fatigue. Because of the failure to eat and the lack of sleep, a patient with untreated tuberculosis disease begins to waste away—which is why the disease was called "consumption." Lung hemorrhages can ultimately lead to death, as they did in the case of Vivien Leigh, the actress who played Scarlett O'Hara in the classic Hollywood movie *Gone with the Wind*.

Eighty-five percent of people who have tuberculosis have disease of the lungs; however, the bacilli can also cause disease of the lymphatic system, the genitourinary tract, and the covering of the brain (meninges), bones, and joints. How the disease progresses is dependent upon many factors including the age of the patient, the presence of coexisting diseases (HIV, diabetes, cancer, or kidney disease, for example), and a history of the BCG vaccination against tuberculosis.

It actually is very difficult for the tubercle bacilli to establish infection and cause disease in a healthy human host. Repeated or prolonged exposure to another person with tuberculosis disease is usually necessary to spread the disease (which may be what happened on the long flight mentioned in the opening paragraph). Individuals who are homeless, living in poverty, are intravenous drug users, or are HIV positive are most susceptible to infection. Poor general health, poor nutrition, other diseases, and overcrowding also contribute to increased host susceptibility and ultimately the development of tuberculosis disease.

The best way to prevent transmission of tuberculosis is to quickly identify infected individuals and provide treatment. Once identified, patients with tuberculosis disease may be hospitalized for treatment. Hospitalized patients should be in private rooms with special air handling and ventilation systems. If infected individuals are treated at home, patients should be very careful around young children or other relatives and acquaintances who fall into the "susceptible" groups previously mentioned. The patient should be taught the proper way to cough and sneeze safely.

It has been known for centuries that coughing and sneezing spread diseases. Before the discovery of bacteria and their association with specific diseases, people understood this, but didn't know why it occurred. The Centers for Disease Control and Prevention recommends that individuals follow a specific procedure when coughing or sneezing in order to prevent the spread of disease microorganisms:[2]

- Cover your mouth and nose with a tissue when you cough or sneeze.
- Put your used tissue in the wastebasket.
- If you don't have a tissue, cough or sneeze into your upper sleeve or elbow, not your hands.
- Wash your hands often with soap and warm water for 20 seconds.
- If soap and water are not available, use an alcohol-based hand rub.

5

Transmission from Organism to Organism

The mortician was shocked when he was diagnosed with tuberculosis. He was not in any high-risk group, had not traveled to a country where the incidence of tuberculosis is high, and had no friends, family, or coworkers with the disease. Where could he have possibly contracted his illness? Could it have been from one of the cadavers he had embalmed? To the mortician's surprise, when the DNA from his tubercle bacilli was compared to the strain of Mycobacterium tuberculosis *that had killed one of the cadavers he had prepared, the strains were identical. It seems the bacteria had become airborne during the embalming process as the fluids that replaced blood moved through the cadaver's mouth and nose. This infusion probably created infectious aerosols that were inhaled by the mortician, resulting in disease.*

A GOOD SNEEZE AND A DEEP COUGH

A good sneeze expels more than 10 million germs; a deep cough expels a similar number. Yet germs or microbes are not released from these actions unprotected. Sneezes and coughs release organisms in drops composed of mucous. Many of the large drops fall to the floor or are inhaled or ingested, where they are rendered harmless by being trapped in nose hairs or swallowed in saliva.

Some of the droplets dry and shrink. These droplets are lightweight and easily carried on tiny air currents far and wide. *Mycobacterium tuberculosis* can float alive for hours or days protected from dehydration by the waxy coating surrounding the organism's cell wall. Dust particles also

Figure 5.1 A sneeze, shown in this stop-action photograph, releases millions of mucous droplets. Bacterial and viral particles from respiratory diseases can be contained in this mucous and travel through the air. Unsuspecting people can inhale these droplets and get sick. This is why it is so important to cover your mouth and nose when you sneeze. (© Bettmann/Corbis)

may trap expelled *Mycobacterium tuberculosis*. When the dust is resuspended by sweeping or by being kicked up, it may pose an infectious threat.

Tuberculosis infection as a result of ingestion of the organism is possible, but is about 10,000 times less effective than infection by inhalation. If the organisms are ingested they are often killed by the highly acidic conditions found in the stomach.

DID YOU KNOW?

According to a recent study, ultraviolet (UV) light may be able to reduce the spread of tuberculosis in hospital wards and waiting rooms by as much as 70%. The research involved quantifying the spread of tuberculosis from infected humans to guinea pigs. According to the World Health Organization, each year more than 9 million people contract tuberculosis and almost 2 million die from it worldwide. The spread of the disease is particularly common in crowded places such as prisons, homeless shelters, and hospitals. The installation of a hanging, shielded UV light from the ceiling with a fan to cir-culate the air will kill the bacteria when they are spread by an infected individual who coughs or sneezes, according to Impe-rial College London, the University of Leeds, Hospital Nacional Dos de Mayo, in Lima, Peru, and a few other research facili-ties. The UV light kills the bacteria, including drug resistant strains, by damaging their DNA so they cannot divide, grow, or infect people. The success of the UV lights is improved by controlling the air flow in the rooms. The fans must direct the UV-treated air downward toward the patients and visitors and bring the infected air upward so that the bacteria are exposed to the lights. The research results were very promising. It was found that 35% of the control group of guinea pigs was infected with tuberculosis from infected humans, but only 9.5% of the guinea pigs in the segment of the study where UV-light-treated air was used became infected.

Source: Imperial College London, "UV Light Cuts Spread of Tuberculosis," *Science Daily*, March 17, 2009, http://www.sciencedaily.com/releases/ 2009/03/090316201505.htm (accessed December 8, 2010).

SPECIAL RISKS TO
HEALTH-CARE WORKERS

Health-care workers are at special risk for being infected with the tubercle bacilli. They are often exposed to undiagnosed tuberculosis patients, and those who work in prisons or shelters may be working under conditions of poor ventilation. Many of the activities that take place in a health-care setting, such as suction and intubation, are likely to produce respiratory aerosols that may contain tubercle bacilli.

In one hospital, during a 45-minute **bronchoscopy**, 13 people assisted with the procedure. Unfortunately, the patient was later found to have tuberculosis. Of the 13 people in the room, 10 became infected by the tubercle bacilli.

Health-care facilities protect their workers by installing special equipment. This equipment includes fans that will exchange the air in a patient's room between six and 12 times an hour and "negative pressure" rooms. Negative pressure prevents air currents from moving from the room into the hallway whenever the door to the room is opened. Rooms should be vented to the outside of the building and the venting tunnels equipped with ultraviolet lights to destroy bacteria that may get into the tunnel. Caregivers also wear special respirators, although recently the use of respirators has become a subject of controversy — not everyone agrees the cost justifies the level of protection gained.

DID YOU KNOW?

From the 1930s to 1960s, research aircraft sampled the air above Earth and found large amounts of seeds and bacteria. A Soviet rocket sampled the atmosphere 40 miles above earth and found bacteria. Clearly, organisms can travel very far on air currents.

TUBERCULOSIS THREATS TO
HUMANS FROM OTHER ANIMALS

Transmission of tubercle bacilli from animals to humans was first recognized in the early 1900s. In the United States, compulsory pasteurization (mild heat treatment of a liquid resulting in the destruction of disease-causing organisms contained within that liquid) was first adopted by Chicago in 1910 and then New York City in 1913. As a result, the public saw a major decrease in the number of children and young adults who developed tuberculosis from consumption of milk contaminated with *Mycobacterium bovis*.

Tuberculosis caused by *Mycobacterium bovis* is clinically identical to that caused by *Mycobacterium tuberculosis*. In countries where animal tuberculosis, particularly cattle tuberculosis, is not controlled, cases of tuberculosis still occur when humans drink or handle contaminated milk. In situations where the organism is ingested, scrofula, intestinal tuberculosis, and other extra-pulmonary forms of tuberculosis are often seen.

No attempts are usually made to determine which species of acid-fast bacilli, either *Mycobacterium tuberculosis* or *Mycobacterium bovis*, has been isolated from the patient's sputum sample. Because *Mycobacterium bovis* is a rare cause of tuberculosis, it requires increased time and expense to correctly identify. Since drug treatment is the same regardless of which species of mycobacteria is causing the disease, public health clinics do not differentiate causes of tuberculosis. Therefore, the number of cases of tuberculosis being transmitted by animals to humans and caused by *Mycobacterium bovis* may currently be underestimated.

Worldwide, *Mycobacterium bovis* causes tuberculosis in a variety of animal species and humans. Annual losses to agriculture are approximately $3 billion. Although pasteurization has virtually eliminated cows as a source of human tuberculosis in the United States and many other nations, in countries where this process is not practiced there are still numerous cases of the disease in the population.[1]

In developed nations, 1 to 2% of human tuberculosis cases are caused by *Mycobacterium bovis*. Unfortunately, in developing nations the technology for culturing and typing needed to make the specific identification of *Mycobacterium bovis* as the causative agent of a case of tuberculosis is often lacking. This leads to inaccurate data concerning the actual number of cases of tuberculosis caused by *Mycobacterium bovis*. Some researchers have speculated that as many as 10 to 15% of new cases of tuberculosis may be caused by this organism in these nations.[2]

In many African countries cattle are an important part of human social life. Cattle in these countries represent wealth, and as such they are at the center of many social events and gatherings. On the continent of Africa, 85 percent of the cattle and 82 percent of the human population live in areas where bovine tuberculosis is only partially controlled or not controlled at all. In addition, pasteurization of milk is rarely practiced in these areas. The lack of tuberculosis control in cattle combined with the regular human exposure to cattle and the high rate of HIV infection in many parts of Africa make tuberculosis transmission from cattle to humans a serious public health concern.

In the United States, animal tuberculosis control and surveillance has been in effect since the early 1900s. In 1918, one of every 20 cattle tested positive for tuberculosis. In 1990, one of every 6,800 tested positive.

Since 1990, federal funds that support research and surveillance of animal tuberculosis in the United States have been severely reduced. Cattle now spend a large amount of time in feedlots before moving onto very large, centrally located slaughterhouses. Many animals that arrive from all over the country and reside in one location for a period of time could give rise to a tuberculosis outbreak.

Table 5.1 Bovine Tuberculosis Cattle Detected at Slaughter and Number of Affected Cattle Herds, United States, 2003–2009*

Final Year	Cattle Positive for *Mycobacterium bovis*, detected at slaughter**	*M. bovis* slaughter cases of foreign origin	*M. bovis* affected herds^	Total domestic population-herds***	Percent herds not affected	Total domestic population-herd***	Percent herd not affected
	(a)	(b)	(c)	(d)	1-(c/d)	(e)	1-((a-b)/e)
2003	38	27	10	1,013,570	99.9990%	96,100,000	99.999989%
2004	36	22	5	989,460	99.9995%	94,888,000	99.999985%
2005	40	27	4	982,510	99.9996%	95,438,000	99.999986%
2006	28	16	9	971,400	99.9991%	96,701,500	99.999988%
2007	24	17	7	967,440	99.9993%	97,002,900	99.999993%
2008	34	25	11	956,500	99.9988%	96,669,000	99.999991%
2009	16	5	12	950,000	99.9987%	94,521,000	99.999988%

* For federal fiscal year ending September 30, 2009.

** Cases are lesioned animals detected at slaughter and laboratory confirmed by polymerase chain reaction or culture to be *Mycobacterium bovis*; each case dose does not necessarily represent a different herd of origin.

*** Source: NASS Agriculture Statistics.

^ Identified through both live animal testing and slaughter surveillance.

Source: United States Department of Agriculture, http://www.aphis.usda.gov/animal_health/animal_diseases/tuberculosis/downloads/tb_erad.pdf (accessed on December 12, 2010).

Between 2003 and 2009, the incidence of tuberculosis infection in cattle in the United States continued to decline to a level where only 16 cattle out of 950,000 were infected.

Mycobacterium bovis can cause tuberculosis in cattle, deer, elk, bison, and goats. Nontraditional animal production of deer, elk, and buffalo, or exotic animal farming of llama and alpacas raises the risk of an animal tuberculosis outbreak. An outbreak within animal herds carries with it the potential for human transmission.

TUBERCULOSIS THREATS TO OTHER ANIMALS FROM HUMANS

In March 1996, five elephants from an exotic animal farm were in California as part of a circus act. One of the elephants died, and upon examination after death, tuberculosis lesions were found in the lungs. Acid-fast bacilli were isolated from the first dead elephant. A second elephant died shortly afterward. That elephant had visible respiratory and trunk exudates. Lung tissue showed caseous necrosis. Of the five elephants, three eventually died from tuberculosis and a fourth was found to be infected with *Mycobacterium tuberculosis.*

Elephant handlers worked closely with the elephants around the clock, and most lived in a building adjacent to the barn where the animals lived. All animal handlers, trainers, and caregivers were given tuberculosis tests, and 50 percent (11 of 22) of the handlers were positive with Mantoux testing. Of the 11 with positive tests, one handler had an X-ray finding suggestive of active tuberculosis. The one handler with active tuberculosis and the remaining infected elephant received multiple drug therapy. The remaining tuberculosis-positive handlers received preventive drug therapy.

Elephants are not known hosts of the tubercle bacilli. Therefore, they must have been infected by one of their handlers. With three of the five elephants dying from tuberculosis, they are clearly a very susceptible animal group and infection is very lethal.

In another case of probable transmission of tuberculosis from humans to animals, a green-winged macaw was ill for several months with occasional loud respiratory sounds, swollen eyelids, poor feeding, diarrhea, and listlessness. The bird lived in an apartment in New York City with several adults for six years. Several months prior to the appearance of these signs, the bird was examined by a veterinarian for rapid breathing. At the time, the bird exhibited several facial lesions that were positive for acid-fast bacilli, but no culture was made. The bird's owner was advised to euthanize it, but the owner chose not to.

When the bird was examined at a large animal hospital in New York City, it presented with multiple nodules on the eyelids of both eyes as well as on the unfeathered areas of its head and face. In addition, there were several nodules on the tongue and glottis seen when the oral cavity was examined. The bird was thin and had a cardiac murmur. X-rays demonstrated an enlarged heart and liver.

The lesions of the eyelids, tongue, and skin were biopsied and revealed the presence of acid-fast bacilli. The bacteria were cultured and, in two weeks, turned out to be *Mycobacterium tuberculosis*. Restriction fragment length polymorphism analysis revealed a three-banded pattern that is the most common pattern in New York City.

The records of the New York City tuberculosis registry were examined and showed that two people with a history of culture-confirmed pulmonary tuberculosis lived at the same address as the parrot's owner. They had a great deal of contact with the bird during the time that they were potentially infectious, which turned out to be three to four years prior to the appearance of the signs in the bird. In fact, they would place food between their lips so the bird could grab it from them. These two people had been treated for tuberculosis before the bird showed any signs of the disease. When the bird showed signs, these two people were tested and found to be free of the disease.

The owner refused to have the bird euthanized after repeated requests from the New York City Health Department. The bird was seized and euthanized under the authority of the New York City Health Code. A necropsy revealed pneumonia, hepatitis (liver inflammation), stomatitis (inflammation of the mouth), glossitis (inflammation of the tongue), myocarditis (inflammation of the heart muscle), endocarditis (inflammation of the inner lining of the heart), and conjunctivitis (inflammation of the mucous membrane that lines the eyeball). Acid-fast bacilli were identified in the lung, liver, and skin lesions. Culturing of these bacilli showed them to be *Mycobacterium tuberculosis*.[3]

The above scenarios bring up an important consideration. How susceptible are animals to tuberculosis spread by humans, and how important is it to protect wildlife from this deadly disease?

With the AIDS epidemic affecting one-third of the population of Botswana, wildlife workers there are particularly concerned about protecting free-ranging wildlife. AIDS and tuberculosis are a common combination, and individuals who have AIDS may shed higher levels of the tubercle bacterium in their sputum. Two reports, an outbreak among banded mongooses and one among **meerkats**, emphasize the danger to wild animals from human tuberculosis. It is believed that both groups of animals contracted the disease by foraging in rubbish heaps outside human homes and a tourist lodge. Once the animals became infected, the disease moved quickly and lethally through their populations.

Ecotourism, travel to unique or pristine ecosystems to observe wildlife, has become very popular in many developing countries. This activity has increased the number of humans coming into contact with wild animals not previously exposed to tuberculosis. It remains to be seen how this increased contact will affect the incidence of airborne human diseases in wild animals.

SPREADING TUBERCULOSIS FROM ONE ANIMAL SPECIES TO ANOTHER

It has been shown that tuberculosis may be spread, not only from animals to humans and from humans to animals, but also from one species of animal to one or several others. In Great Britain, there has been an increasing problem relating to the spread of tuberculosis (*Mycobacterium bovis*) to cattle by badgers (*Meles meles*). It appears that badgers are a reservoir for the disease in that they may be infected, but rarely succumb to the disease. However, they are an effective source of transmission of tuberculosis to domesticated cattle.

According to Britain's Department for Environment, Food, and Rural Affairs (DEFRA), bovine tuberculosis is endemic in some areas of Great Britain and is increasing at a rate of 18% per year. Approximately 20,000 infected cows are destroyed annually, causing financial hardships to many farmers.[4]

It is assumed that the badger-to-badger spread of tuberculosis is accomplished via aerosol transmission. However, the mode of transmission from badgers to cattle is less clear. Scientists assume that the major route is via scent marks, particularly in urine. Badger feces and pus also contain high numbers of bacteria. Therefore, cattle that graze on grass along the periphery of fields are at a greater risk of contracting tuberculosis as this is where badgers are more prone to scent. The risk is increased by the badgers' behavioral trait of taking very precise routes and marking these areas repeatedly. In addition to badgers, ferrets and red foxes have also been suspected of being vectors for the transmission of *Mycobacterium bovis*.

In the United States, deer in Michigan have been shown to be infected with *Mycobacterium bovis*. They apparently became

infected with the bacteria due to humans feeding them, attract-
ing large congregations of deer in small areas. The disease
spread among the deer due to close contact and eventually
spread from the deer to grazing adult cattle. Nursing calves
contract the disease by drinking bacteria-infected milk from
their mother.[5]

6

The Immune Response to Tuberculosis Infection

Barbara was a 20-year-old college senior who had come to the United States from Europe to study at a prestigious university. Her goal in life was to become a medical doctor and help people in any way that she could.

She had always been a healthy girl and rarely suffered with any illnesses. The worst she suffered was an occasional cold. One day, out of nowhere, she went totally blind. She was more frightened than she had ever been. She immediately was taken to a doctor who began tests to determine the cause of the blindness. The next day her vision returned as quickly as it had disappeared. The doctor didn't like this at all, as this type of occurrence is often associated with multiple sclerosis (MS). He was awaiting the results of his tests before he made a definitive diagnosis.

In the meantime, Barbara began to develop muscle weakness and blurry vision, also symptoms of MS. Now she was beside herself with fear and worry. What would she do if the diagnosis was, indeed, MS? Sadly, the doctor confirmed the existence of the typical neurological changes associated with the disease and confirmed the diagnosis.

There was, however, one very interesting finding that came up during all of the testing. Barbara also had Mycobacterium tuberculosis *in her ovaries and her bones. Although she had never been diagnosed with pulmonary tuberculosis, the bacteria were in her body. The doctor explained that, perhaps, she had had a case of tuberculosis as a child in Europe, but it was not diagnosed and her immune system was able to keep it in check. However, since MS is thought to be an autoimmune disease in which the body's immune system begins to attack the myelin insulation along the nerves, the immune system became primed by the tuberculosis infection and was hyperactivated, thus causing the multiple sclerosis. There was no proof of this, but it was not out of the realm of possibility.*

Tuberculosis fights a war with the body, and the lungs are often the battlefield. On one side is the organism with its artillery and maneuvers, attempting to establish itself in the host for the long term. As with all parasites, the idea is not to kill the host, which would be self-defeating because the host provides the parasite with resources necessary for its survival, but only to dominate. On the opposing side is the host immune response. The first wave of troops includes the nonspecific response ready to handle any invader. That initial defense is followed by the specific host immune response whose sole focus is to eliminate the specific organism causing the problem. The immune response seeks to take no prisoners. It is an all-out war bent on eliminating the invader at all costs, even if some collateral damage ends up destroying host tissues.

EARLY BATTLES

Once *Mycobacterium tuberculosis* reaches the lungs, patrolling lung macrophages ingest the bacteria (Figure 6.1). This ingestion occurs when the phagocytic cell engulfs the organism by sending out pseudopods (armlike projections) to surround the bacterium. The ingested bacteria become enclosed inside the macrophage in a membrane-bound vacuole called the **phagosome**.

THE HOST CELL ARSENAL

Within the phagocytic cell are **lysosomes**, which contain various lytic enzymes meant to destroy invading parties. When a lysosome fuses with a phagosome, a **phagolysosome** forms, and the contents of the lysosome are free to destroy the engulfed bacteria.

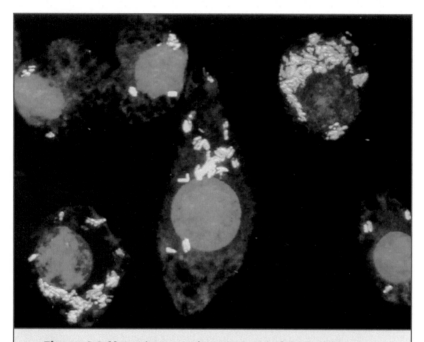

Figure 6.1 Macrophages, an important part of the body's defense system, ingest foreign invaders in an attempt to prevent disease. In this picture, macrophages have ingested the tuberculosis bacilli. The macrophages are stained fluorescent green (the nucleus of each macrophage glows brighter than the rest of the cell), and the bacteria are stained fluorescent orange. Techniques such as fluorescent staining are often used to help scientists visualize cellular processes in the body. (Center for Tuberculosis Research, Johns Hopkins University)

Inside the macrophage, a respiratory burst may occur, resulting in the release of oxygen-containing molecules (such as hydrogen peroxide) that also have the potential to destroy the bacteria. The macrophage can release various proteins and peptides that kill organisms, polyamines that combine with other compounds to form deadly hydrogen peroxide or ammonia, or iron chelators that make iron unavailable to the bacteria. Iron plays a key role in the process of bacterial respiration. Without iron, the bacteria cannot produce enough ATP (the fuel of the cell) and, as a result, death occurs.

THE BACTERIUM FIGHTS BACK

For every attack of the immune system, there is a counterattack by the organism. The tubercle bacilli can prevent fusion of the lysosome and phagosome, although the exact mechanism by which this occurs is unknown. It has been proposed that ammonia (a base with a pH above 7) generated by mycobacterial urease neutralizes phagosomal pH (usually mildly acidic with a pH of approximately 6.2) causing inhibition of phagosome-lysosome fusion. Keep in mind that on the pH scale, which ranges from 0 to 14, a pH of 7 is neutral whereas any pH below 7 is acidic and any pH above 7 is basic.[1]

If fusion does take place, some organisms may be able to escape the phagolysosome itself. *Mycobacterium tuberculosis* can release molecules that render toxic forms of oxygen harmless. These enzymes, **superoxide dismutase** and **catalase**, are normally used by the organism in any oxygen-containing environment. The organism can release substances that stimulate the macrophage to deactivate itself, making it ineffective in battle. Physical components of the bacterium, such as cord factor, may also be toxic to macrophages.

DID YOU KNOW?

What Is a Cytokine or a Lymphokine?

Both **cytokines** and **lymphokines** are regulatory molecules that cells produce to communicate with one another. They often function to increase the intensity of the specific immune response. Cytokines are produced by macrophages, natural killer cells, mast cells, and others. Lymphokines are special cytokines produced only by lymphocytes.

Tubercle Lesion

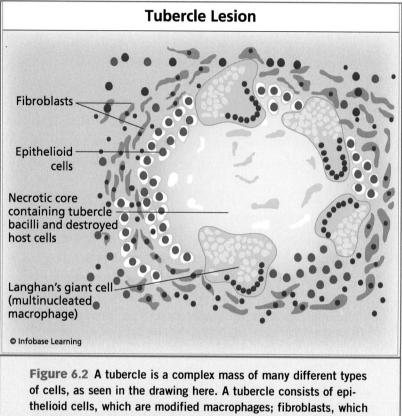

Fibroblasts

Epithelioid cells

Necrotic core containing tubercle bacilli and destroyed host cells

Langhan's giant cell (multinucleated macrophage)

© Infobase Learning

Figure 6.2 A tubercle is a complex mass of many different types of cells, as seen in the drawing here. A tubercle consists of epithelioid cells, which are modified macrophages; fibroblasts, which are host cells; and giant cells (multinucleated cells resulting from macrophage fusion). At the center of the tubercle are bacteria and the caseous necrosis that results from enzymatic destruction of host cells.

Very virulent tuberculosis bacteria cause the macrophage to burst, releasing organisms into the surrounding tissues. The released bacteria may be taken up by immature macrophages, too naïve or weak to kill the ingested organisms.

Waves of macrophages bursting, release of tuberculosis bacteria, and ingestion by weak macrophages give rise to the tubercle lesion, known generically as a **granuloma**, which begins to enlarge. Other immune cells such as **monocytes** are recruited to the area by cytokines (a process known as chemotaxis). These monocytes can transform into dendritic cells that also contribute to formation of the tubercle. These dendritic cells process antigenic information and present it on their surface to other cells of the immune system. The cells are found in areas that are in contact with the external environment, such as the nose and lungs, digestive system, and skin. The tubercle encapsulates, or walls off, the bacteria, effectively reducing the available oxygen for the organisms. Organisms will begin to reproduce slowly, if at all, in the lesion.

THE COUNTERATTACK

In the meantime, the specific immune response is marshaled and T lymphocytes, also called T cells, begin to arrive. Macrophages that have been successful at killing bacteria activate T cells. These activated T cells secrete lymphokines, which affect other cells and tissues in many ways.

Table 6.1 **Important Cytokines, Their Sources, and Functions Involved in the Host Response to Tuberculosis Infection**

Cytokine Name	Source	Action
Interferon gamma	T lymphocyte and natural killer cells	Activates macrophages
Interleukin 1	Macrophage, epithelial cells	Proliferates T lymphocytes; promotes macrophage production of cytokines
Interleukin 6	T lymphocytes, macrophage	Promotes T and B lymphocyte growth
Interleukin 10	Macrophage, mast cells	Decreases rate of reproduction of T lymphocytes; promotes antibody production
Interleukin 12	Macrophage	Activates natural killer cells; influences T cells to release other cytokines
Tumor necrosis	T lymphocyte	Activates primed macrophage factor and natural killer cells; stimulates cytotoxic T lymphocytes

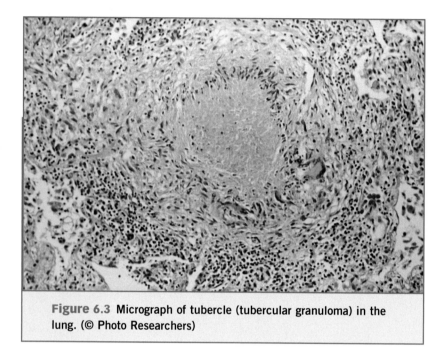

Figure 6.3 Micrograph of tubercle (tubercular granuloma) in the lung. (© Photo Researchers)

Some of the activated T cells may be cytotoxic, or killers of other cells. Cytotoxic T cells attack and destroy host macrophages that have ingested tuberculosis bacilli. Uninfected host cells may be accidentally destroyed by the large concentration of cytokines released at this point.

If the actions of T cells and macrophages can control the progression of the lesions and the spread of bacilli, the disease will be arrested. The key battle strategy of the specific immune response is to destroy organisms wherever they may be before their numbers get too high. As a consequence, more tissue damage and cell destruction may be prevented.

THE BATTLE LOST

If the immune response is unsuccessful and the bacterial concentration gets too high, then **liquefaction** of the tubercle will result. During liquefaction, the tubercle degrades because host cells that make up the structure are destroyed by the massive release of cell-destroying enzymes from other host cells. Once the lesion becomes liquefied, bacteria are no longer contained in phagocytic cells and begin to multiply uncontrollably. The bacteria multiply robustly because the concentration of oxygen is greater outside the phagocytic cell than inside. If the liquid spills into a nearby bronchiole, a cavity results. This cavity can be seen on an X-ray and provides clues when diagnosing tuberculosis disease. In the meantime, bacilli that have gained free access to the bronchii may be released during a cough and infect other victims.

A STALEMATE

If the number of bacteria remains low enough to be contained by the tubercle, the host immune response will subside, and the combatants reach a stalemate. The bacteria remain sequestered inside the lesion. This situation (latent tuberculosis) may last throughout the life of the victim. If something should happen to change the immune status of the host, such as HIV infection, an organ transplant, or steroid therapy for arthritis, this latent or arrested disease may reactivate.

Approximately 60 million people around the world have active tuberculosis, so it would seem that the immune system is outmatched against the tuberculosis bacterium. Yet given that an estimated 1.7 billion people worldwide may have been infected without developing the active disease, the host immune response must be winning more wars than the organism.

7

Screening for and Diagnosis of Tuberculosis

The new students who had been accepted to the college were eager to begin their studies and get degrees that they could use to make their marks on the world. Of course, in order to attend classes they all had to pass physical exams, be up to date with their vaccinations, and be healthy and ready to work.

One of the required tests was a Mantoux test, in which a purified protein derivative from Mycobacterium tuberculosis *is injected under the skin in order to detect the presence of antibodies in the blood of the individual being tested. The presence of these antibodies indicates that the person is either suffering from an active case of tuberculosis, had one in the past, or has been exposed to the bacteria in one way or another.*

Of the 500 entering students who were tested, only one developed a raised red bump at the site of the injection. The school physicians recognized this as a positive response and immediately told the student to have a chest X-ray and find out if an active lung infection with Mycobacterium tuberculosis *was occurring.*

The X-ray showed no signs of an active infection, but it did reveal a few small scars in the student's lungs. These were determined to be sites of old tuberculosis infections from the boy's childhood. As it turned out, he had emigrated to the United States from Africa, where tuberculosis exists in high numbers. He had most likely had been infected and was able to get over it. A course of antibiotic treatment was begun, and he was allowed to attend classes.

In his search for a cure for tuberculosis, Dr. Koch observed that animals infected with tuberculosis developed a lesion at the site of inoculation if a substance called tuberculin was injected. Tuberculin, or old tuberculin as it is now known, was prepared from filtered, heat-sterilized cultures of *Mycobacterium tuberculosis*. Before use, the filtrate was evaporated to 10% of its original volume. While this concentrate proved to be of no value in preventing tuberculosis, several scientists of the time felt the reaction observed could be of some value as a screening tool to identify those people that had been exposed to the organism.

THE SEARCH FOR A SPECIFIC, REPRODUCIBLE SCREENING TOOL

One of those scientists, Austrian physician Clemens von Pirquet, first used the term **allergy** (from the Greek *allos ergos*, meaning *altered energy*) to describe a positive reaction to old tuberculin. He used the word **anergy** (Greek for *without energy*) to describe the lack of reaction to old tuberculin. The term *anergy* is often found today in information describing the lack of response to tuberculin testing by immuno-compromised individuals.

As researchers searched for the best way to use tuberculin as a screening tool in the early 1900s, one French physician, **Charles Mantoux**, introduced the technique of inoculating tuberculin just below the skin. This method of screening, developed in 1908 and known as the Mantoux test, is the preferred method of screening in use today. Although the Mantoux technique of screening was widely accepted, there were still some problems with preparation of old tuberculin, which at times proved unreliable due to its heterogeneous nature and non-specificity.

MODIFYING OLD TUBERCULIN MAKES ITS USE MORE RELIABLE

In 1934, **Florence Seibert**, who worked at the Phipps Institute in Philadelphia, developed a technique to extract proteins from *Mycobacterium tuberculosis* after it was grown on culture media and killed by heating to 121°C at 15 pounds of air pressure (a process known as autoclaving). Her preparation, which came to be known as **purified protein derivative (PPD)**, allowed standardization of the product used for testing and provided specific and reproducible results. Other than the addition of a detergent to prolong shelf life, Dr. Seibert's formulation of PPD is used today to screen for tuberculosis.

WHAT IS THE TEST DETECTING?

When tuberculin is injected into someone who has been exposed to *Mycobacterium tuberculosis*, a reaction will occur at the injection site (Arthus reaction). This reaction, which remains local, occurs because phagocytic cells and sensitized T lymphocytes (sensitive because of previous exposure to the organism) migrate to the area. Once at the site of inoculation, the cells that have migrated release chemicals that create an inflammatory reaction. Local activity of the phagocytic cells and other inflammatory cells causes a lack of oxygen and acidic conditions in the area that can lead to host tissue destruction. All of these activities take place in a 48- to 72-hour period. For that reason this response is called a **delayed hypersensitivity reaction**.

The first time this type of reaction was demonstrated was in 1903 when Nicolas Maurice Arthus demonstrated that by subcutaneously injecting horse serum repeatedly into rabbits, edema (tissue swelling) and redness developed at the site of the injection. The reason for this response is the activation of complement antibodies and the migration of neutrophils to the injection site causing a localized **inflammation** of small blood vessels (vasculitis) and an overall inflammatory response in the tissue.

In order to interpret the results, the reaction at the inoculation site is observed and measured. The resulting measurements are interpreted in conjunction with other identified risk factors.

Table 7.1 **Interpreting Mantoux Tuberculin Skin Test Results**
The following measurement guide for interpreting the Mantoux tuber-culin skin test identifies individuals who may have been exposed to tuberculosis. The following measurements of induration (skin wheal) reaction) are classified as positive, based on individual risk factors.

Induration (Skin Wheal) Diameter	Individual Risk Factors
≥ 5mm	Positive Test Result For: • Persons with HIV infection • Recent contacts of persons with active TB disease • Persons with evidence of old, healed TB lesions on chest X-rays • Persons with organ transplants and other immunosuppressed persons, including those receiving prolonged corticosteroid therapy (the equivalent of >15mg/d of prednisone for one month or more) and TNF-a blockers
≥ 10mm	Positive Test Result For: • Persons who have immigrated within the past five years from areas with high TB rates* • Injection drug users • Persons who live or work in institutional settings where exposure to TB may be likely, such as hospitals, prisons, homeless shelters, and nursing homes • Mycobacteriology laboratory personnel • Persons with clinical conditions associated with increased risk of progression to active TB, including: silicosis; chronic renal failure; diabetes; more than 10% below ideal weight or BMI < 18.5; gastrectomy/jejunoileal bypass; some hematologic disorders (such as leukemia and lymphomas); and certain cancers (such as carcinoma of the head, neck, or lung, leukemias, and lymphomas) • Children under five, and children or adolescents exposed to adults in high-risk categories • Persons with prolonged stay in areas with high TB rates*
≥ 15mm	Positive Test Result For: • Persons at low risk for active TB disease for whom testing is not generally indicated

* Countries with high rates of TB include China, Dominican Republic, Ecuador, Haiti, Honduras, India, Mexico, Pakistan, Peru, Philippines, South Korea, and all of Africa.

Source: New York City Department of Health and Mental Hygiene, "The Mantoux Tuberculin Skin Test: A Guide for Providers," available at http://www.nyc.gov/html/doh/downloads/pdf/tb/tb-hcp-tst-guide.pdf (accessed December 16, 2010).

HOW IS THE TEST DONE?

Tuberculin may be delivered in one of two ways: either by a multiple puncture device (a **tine test**) or by injecting a specific amount under the skin (the Mantoux test).

The multiple puncture device has multiple tines (4–6) that introduce tuberculin in a pattern into the skin. These devices usually consist of a plastic handle attached to a stainless steel disk. Projecting from the disk are metal prongs about two mm in length. One type of multiple puncture device includes a spring-loaded gun with sterile cartridges that deliver liquid tuberculin. When multiple puncture devices are used, they must be in contact with the skin for at least one second. The reaction produced should be measured in 48 to 72 hours. The patient may be given a card showing possible reaction outcomes in order to make test interpretation easier.

Advantages of using the tine test are: ease of administration, stability of the preparation, and short administration time.

DID YOU KNOW?

What Is Inflammation?

Inflammation is the body's response to tissue injury or invasion by a foreign substance. In the process of inflammation, damaged or invaded host tissue releases chemical signals that attract phagocytic cells and other immune cells to the area. These phagocytic cells ingest the invader, while the other immune cells release chemicals called cytokines to recruit more immune cells. Resulting from all this activity are the four classical indications of inflammation: redness, heat, swelling, and pain. Inflammation should be considered a good thing because it is the body's attempt to eliminate the invader and repair the damage. Sometimes, however, it can be an overzealous response and result in host tissue damage, as in the case of hypersensitivity or allergic reactions.

Disadvantages include problems standardizing the amount of tuberculin delivered, difficulty controlling the depth of the puncture, and the time the device is in contact with the skin.

Because of the variation of results in large screening programs, the American Academy of Pediatrics recommends that the tine test no longer be used to screen children.

THE MANTOUX TEST

It is now recommended that all screening for tuberculosis be done using the Mantoux method. In this technique, five **TU**s (tuberculin units, 0.1µg of PPD delivered in 0.1 ml of liquid) are delivered just under the skin using a short, blunt needle.

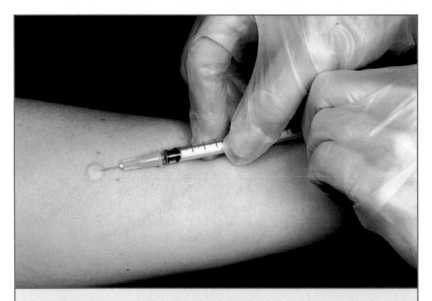

Figure 7.1 The Mantoux test, shown here, is used to test for tuberculosis. A short, blunt needle is used to deliver purified protein derivative (PPD) just under the skin, and a small wheal, or bubble, should appear on the surface of the skin. The area where the test is administered is evaluated in 48–72 hours. A hard raised bump indicates a positive test. (Centers for Disease Control and Prevention)

The injection is usually made on the underside of the forearm by placing the needle, flat side up, into the skin at a shallow angle. As the fluid is delivered, it should produce a **wheal**, a pale fluid-filled bubble 6–10 millimeters (mm) in size just under the skin. This bubble will eventually disappear and the area should be evaluated in 48 to 72 hours.

INTERPRETATION OF THE REACTION

Test results should be interpreted between 48 and 72 hours after the test is performed. When interpreting the results, only the hard raised area, called the **induration**, should be measured. Any redness surrounding the induration should not be included in the measurement. Although Mantoux described a positive

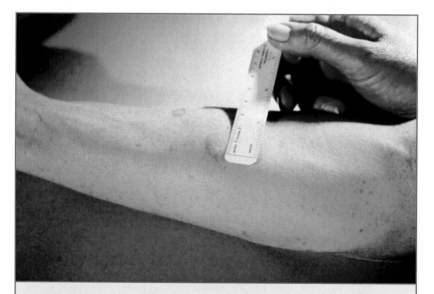

Figure 7.2 After delivery of either the tine or the Mantoux test, the injection site must be evaluated for the presence of a bump. The bump is usually measured with a ruler, and the size of the reaction will indicate a positive test. The size necessary for a positive test varies. (Centers for Disease Control and Prevention)

test as being the size of a two franc coin, we now know that the measurements mean different things for different at-risk groups.

For an individual who has no known risk factors for contracting tuberculosis, an induration measuring 15 millimeters or more indicates exposure to *Mycobacterium tuberculosis* or latent infection. It does not mean the individual has active tuberculosis disease. Additional tests and observations should be made before reaching that conclusion.

An induration zone of 10 mm or more should be considered positive for individuals who fall into the following high-risk groups:

- IV drug users
- Non-United States born persons from high-risk areas such as Asia, Africa, and Latin America
- An individual who has suffered a weight loss greater than 10% of body weight
- Children exposed to adults at high risk
- Individuals with medical risk factors including diabetes, cancer, and kidney disease
- Residents of long-term care facilities (prisons, nursing homes, psychiatric facilities)
- Health-care workers and employees who provide services to any of the above mentioned groups.

An induration measuring 5 mm or more should be considered positive for individuals in the following groups:

- HIV-positive individuals
- Individuals with chest X-rays consistent with healed tuberculosis lesions
- Individuals in recent contact with others who have active diagnosed tuberculosis
- Individuals undergoing therapy that suppresses their immune system, such as organ transplant recipients.

BEYOND SCREENING

If an individual has a positive response to the screening test, additional steps should be taken to confirm the diagnosis. The patient should be screened for clinical signs and symptoms typically associated with tuberculosis disease. These include cough, fever, failure to gain weight, or weight loss. Forms of tuberculosis other than pulmonary tuberculosis may manifest themselves with different signs and symptoms.

Chest X-rays should be performed to look for changes in lung tissue and enlargement of lymph nodes in the area. If the chest X-ray is abnormal or the patient has a cough, sputum cultures should be obtained to look for acid-fast bacteria.

Typically, once a sputum sample is collected it must be smeared on a slide and stained using acid-fast technique to determine if *Mycobacterium tuberculosis* is present. For a definitive identification, the sample must be cultured in the laboratory and further examined after bacteria have grown. Because *Mycobacterium tuberculosis* is a slow-growing bacterium, this procedure can take two to four weeks to complete for a positive identification.

Recently, a rapid identification technique was developed that is able to accurately diagnose a case of tuberculosis in a patient in 90 minutes. The test is called Xpert MTB/RIF and is able to identify the bacteria in 98% of cases as well as detecting whether or not the bacteria are resistant to rifampicin, which is a first-line drug to treat the disease. In addition, a single test is able to diagnose tuberculosis in 72% of those patients infected with both HIV and tuberculosis. Currently, the techniques used for *Mycobacterium tuberculosis* are less reliable in these patients.[1]

It is up to the physician to decide when to begin antibiotic treatment. For patients who belong to the high-risk groups, the doctor may begin antibiotic therapy before the diagnosis is conclusive. In the case of some high-risk individuals, much host damage could occur if the patient is not treated immediately.

COMPLICATIONS AND DRAWBACKS OF TESTING

Adverse reactions to the screening tests are rare. However, upon repeated testing, nonresponders (no initial reaction to Mantoux testing) may produce induration, a phenomenon known as **boosting**. There may be some variability in response to tuberculin depending upon the immune status of the host. For example, AIDS patients rarely respond to screening although they may have active tuberculosis. These individuals are anergic because they have a limited (if any) T cell population.

Anyone who has been vaccinated with BCG will usually have a reaction to the screening test even if they have not been exposed to *Mycobacterium tuberculosis*. People infected with nontuberculosis mycobacteria may also produce a positive reaction.

Nontuberculous mycobacteria (NTM) include those that do not cause tuberculosis or leprosy (*Mycobacterium leprae* and *Mycobacterium lepromatosis*). These are often environmental and are commonly found in streams, marshes, wet soil, estuaries, and rivers. These bacteria are not transmitted from animals to humans or from humans to humans and are usually acquired from environmental contact.[2]

DID YOU KNOW?

Is It Spit or Sputum?

It is important when looking for acid-fast bacteria to have the right sample. If you are asked for a sputum sample, be sure you do not provide spit. What is the difference? Spit is saliva and material from the mouth, whereas sputum is material coughed up from the lung. In the case of tuberculosis, sputum will contain acid-fast bacteria, spit will not.

As with *Mycobacterium tuberculosis*, the most common manifestation of an infection with NTM is pulmonary disease. Other clinical indications include infections throughout the body, in skin and soft tissue, and in the lymphatic system. The pulmonary form of the disease is most often seen in post-menopausal women, patients with underlying lung diseases, AIDS, or cancer.[3]

Diseases associated with NTM are seen more often in industrialized nations than in those that are less technologically advanced. The incidence rate in these countries is 1–1.8 per 100,000 or possibly higher. Some researchers estimate that pulmonary cases of NTM may be 10 times more common than tuberculosis in the United States, with possibly 150,000 cases per year occurring. Non-pulmonary cases have been identified via the LASIK procedure (laser-assisted in situ keratomileusis) used to correct nearsightedness, farsightedness and astigmatism, and to the use of urinary catheters.[4]

8

The BCG Vaccine

Dominique had been accepted to work at a major hospital as a registered nurse. She was very excited about being able to get a job so quickly following her arrival in New York from Haiti, where she had done her training and had worked as a nurse for several years. She was all set to get started as soon as the preliminary testing was done to be sure that she was healthy.

She was examined by a physician at the hospital and given the required PPD shot. A few days later, when the doctor examined the site of the injection, he noticed a raised red bump. This was an indication that there were tubercular proteins in her bloodstream and that she was exposed to Mycobacterium tuberculosis. The human resources director called her into his office on the day before she was to begin her shift. He looked rather distressed as he told her that she would be unable to start work the next day because her PPD test was positive.

Because Dominique came from Haiti, she had been vaccinated with BCG vaccine when she was born. She had never had a case of tuberculosis. She explained this to the personnel director, but to no avail. Dominique was required to take a regimen of antibiotics used to treat tuberculosis and get a chest X-ray. The X-ray was negative, but she still had to take the antibiotics before she was allowed to start working at the hospital. She did as she was told and eventually began working as a nurse. Within a few years, the hospital realized that this was happening with all of their foreign employees and allowed them to continue working as long as the chest X-ray was negative.

More people in the world are vaccinated against one particular infectious disease than any other. Is it polio, tetanus, measles, chicken pox, or hepatitis? Actually, more humans are alive today that have been vaccinated against tuberculosis than any other disease, yet most people in the United States have not received the vaccine, let alone ever heard of it. Although administered for the past 80 years, this stable, safe, and relatively inexpensive vaccine remains controversial.

HISTORY OF BCG

In the early 1900s, **Albert Calmette** and **Camille Guérin** were working at the Pasteur Institute in Lille, France. In 1906, Calmette observed that guinea pigs seemed to be protected from tuberculosis disease when they were first fed a horse strain (weakly infectious in humans) of the tubercle bacilli and then infected with a more virulent strain of the organism. Calmette and Guérin then began to study *Mycobacterium bovis*, a close relative of *Mycobacterium tuberculosis* that can also cause the disease in human beings. They had trouble with the organism clumping during growth, so they added ox bile to their potato-based growth media in hopes of changing the culture characteristics of the organism.

Calmette and Guérin were familiar with the techniques of Louis Pasteur, the institute's namesake, who attenuated (weakened) the ability of viruses to cause disease by serial passage in a host. He created an early rabies vaccine by serially passing the virus from rabbit to rabbit. This serial passage involved infecting rabbits with rabies, allowing the virus to incubate for a while, sacrificing the infected rabbits and drying their spinal cords, which is where the virus ends up residing. The next group of rabbits was infected using the dried spinal cord tissue. The procedure was repeated several times and the virus mutated into a weakened form that Pasteur used as a vaccine, first in dogs and then in humans.

They sought to follow in the footsteps of Pasteur, so they transferred their strain of *Mycobacterium bovis* many times (231 times, over the course of 13 years) in media until the organism could no longer cause disease (as a byproduct, it also no longer clumped).

Calmette and Guérin spent the next several years infecting cattle, guinea pigs, monkeys, pigs, and chimps, and showed that their strain, BCG (Bacille Calmette Guérin), did not revert to one that could cause disease. In 1921, they received the opportunity to try the vaccine on humans. Calmette and Guérin administered their BCG strain to a newborn whose mother had died of tuberculosis. The child's grandmother, with whom she would live, also had the disease. The newborn received the vaccine on the third, fifth, and seventh days after birth. The vaccine proved to be a success! There were no harmful side effects,

Figure 8.1 Albert Calmette, pictured here, worked with Camille Guérin to develop a tuberculosis vaccine. They continually grew a strain of tuberculosis until it was no longer infectious, and then used that strain to infect animals. This led to their discovery of a human tuberculosis vaccine, which is still used in several countries throughout the world, although not in the United States. (© Bettmann/Corbis)

and the child remained free of tuberculosis for the rest of her life. Over the next six years, 969 children were vaccinated. Only 3.9 percent of them died from tuberculosis or other causes. Use of the vaccine gained public as well as governmental support, culminating in the recommendation of BCG for use against tuberculosis by the League of Nations in 1928.

Unfortunately, a major catastrophe involving use of the vaccine occurred in 1929 in Germany. Two hundred fifty-two children were vaccinated, of whom 72 died. Later it was discovered that a mistake was made at the lab that prepared the vaccine. Somehow, a disease-causing strain had contaminated the culture that was used to make vaccine. Although the mistake was found and the BCG vaccine vindicated, in the public opinion, damage was done. Albert Calmette took this failure personally, and, it is said, as a result he died a disheartened man in 1933.

CURRENT VACCINE PRODUCTION

The World Health Organization currently oversees production and distribution of the tuberculosis vaccine. Seven different strains of the organism are now used around the world to produce the vaccine. These strains are named for the locations of the laboratories in which they are grown. They are BCG (Paris), BCG (Copenhagen), BCG (TICE–University of Illinois), BCG (Montreal), BCG (Russia/Bulgaria), BCG (Japan), and BCG (Connaught–Czech Republic). The factors that make one strain different from another are variations in molecular and genetic characteristics. Whether one strain is any better than another at imparting immunity to a vaccinated individual is unclear.

Although the seven strains were derived from the original strain of Calmette and Guérin, the organisms have since been grown under different conditions and in different laboratories. These different cultural conditions have given rise to mutations in the strains resulting in differences in appearance, ability to grow and survive, rate of growth, and ability to induce an immune response in the host.

To produce the vaccine, the organism is grown on the surface of liquid media for six to nine days. The organism is then harvested and the resulting clump is broken up into a homogeneous suspension. The preparation is freeze-dried and resuspended in either saline or distilled water. To avoid further differences in strains and to attempt to maintain production quality, no original stock culture each laboratory possesses is to be transferred more than 12 times.

SAFETY OF BCG

Limited side effects occur following vaccination. Some induration and ulceration at the vaccine site may be seen, and a vaccine scar may form as a result of inoculation. Other, more serious side effects have been reported in varying percentages in individuals who were vaccinated. These include painful urination, urinary frequency, blood in the urine, urinary tract infection, feelings of malaise (general body weakness or discomfort), anemia, nausea and vomiting, fever, and chills. Severe neurological and other fatal complications resulting from vaccination are very rare. It is important to note that HIV-positive individuals should not receive the vaccine as they may actually develop disseminated (occurring throughout the body) tuberculosis infection due to the weakness of their immune systems. The United States remains one of the few industrialized nations not to use BCG on a national scale.

HOW WELL DOES THE VACCINE
PROTECT AGAINST TUBERCULOSIS?

Although safe and relatively inexpensive, the effectiveness of the vaccine remains a topic of considerable debate. Studies of vaccinated groups report effectiveness ranging from zero to 75 percent, with an average of 50 percent effectiveness in preventing tuberculosis. These differences in protective rates may be due to variation in vaccine production, vaccine administration, gender of the recipient, genetic differences of populations, age of the recipient, nutrition, socioeconomic status, history of previous exposure, stage of diagnosis, and follow-up after vaccination.

Although the exact percentage of effectiveness continues to be debated, most researchers agree that the vaccine works best in children, providing better than 80 percent protection against serious forms of the disease. The vaccine provides more protection against disseminated disease than pulmonary disease. Recent reports have suggested that the vaccine may provide some cross-protection against leprosy, a disease caused by *Mycobacterium leprae*.

THE SEARCH FOR NEW VACCINES

Given the debate over BCG and the uneven immune response produced as a result of vaccination, emphasis is currently being placed on the development of new vaccines. With the sequencing of the *Mycobacterium tuberculosis* genome, it is hoped that genes associated with virulence can and will be identified. Once identified, these genes could be deleted, creating attenuated strains of bacteria, which could be used as a vaccine that would produce effective host immunity but not harm the host.

A team of medical investigators, led by Dr. Douglas Kernodle at Vanderbilt University Medical Center in Tennessee, was successful at discovering why the BCG vaccine has been losing its effectiveness in imparting immunity against pulmonary tuberculosis. It is still 80% effective in preventing disseminated tuberculosis in early childhood and it is administered annually to approximately 100 million newborns worldwide outside of the United States.[1]

During the past 60 years, medical scientists believed that the attenuated *Mycobacterium bovis* used in manufacturing the BCG vaccine was losing its ability to impart immunity because it had become too attenuated due to the numerous serial passages it had undergone. According to Dr. Kernodle, the belief was that it had become too "wimpy" to do the job.

Kernodle's team investigated the reason why BCG actually lost its effectiveness from a different approach. In 2001, they suggested that *Mycobacterium tuberculosis* evades the immune system by producing antioxidants that act to suppress the host's immune system, thus allowing the bacteria to get a strong foothold and bring about an infection. The team felt that by taking something away from BCG, thus attenuating it even further, they could be successful in making the vaccine an even better immune system stimulant. Of course, this thinking was completely opposed to that of the majority of the scientific community.

Nevertheless, they pursued this line of reasoning in their research and in 2007 they modified the BCG and began to test it for its ability to produce an immune response. At the same time, researchers at the Pasteur Institute in Paris did a genomic analysis of BCG and found that, in addition to containing the gene deletions that were directly responsible for the bacteria's attenuation, there were also regions of gene duplication and expression that were related to the production of more antioxidants. Thanks to this research, Kernodle's team realized that they were right and that these mutated bacteria were even better at suppressing the immune system due to their ability to produce more antioxidants.

More recent research by the team, this time spearheaded by Dr. Lakshmi Sadagopal, involved vaccinating mice with a genetically modified strain of BCG that reduced or eliminated the production of several antioxidants. After the initial dose of vaccine was administered, a second "challenge" dose was given to the mice several days later. Dr. Sadagopal discovered that, compared to the standard BCG vaccine, the modified version induced a more powerful immune response and a better recall response in addition to being eliminated more effectively by the immune system. The team felt that these results might correlate with an improved vaccine in humans. Additionally, they believed that they were able to develop a vaccine that is more like that of the 1920s when it was first introduced and was 80% effective against pulmonary tuberculosis.

A further step in creating a very effective vaccine would be to genetically engineer the bacteria to produce even fewer or less-active antioxidants than are produced by naturally occurring strains of BCG. The Aeras Global TB Vaccine Foundation, with the help of a grant from the Bill and Melinda Gates Foundation, has licensed the modification technology that was developed by Kernodle's team in India, South Africa, and Kenya. These are areas of the world with a high incidence of tuberculosis.

Genomics can also provide clues as to the nature of the antigens that induce a host immune response. These antigens could then be cloned in a noninfectious bacterium and used in a vaccine to produce immunity. A vaccine of this kind would be compatible with tuberculin testing that is currently done in the United States because it would not interfere with test outcome.

Several different candidate vaccines are currently under investigation. The modes of action associated with each of these differ from the standard mode used with the BCG vaccine and most others. One type involves live mycobacterial vaccines that are created either by adding genes that make the vaccine more effective or by removing genes that help the bacteria to be virulent, such as the modified BCG vaccine noted above. This procedure is referred to as recombination. Preclinical studies have shown that two of these vaccines are more effective and safer than the standard BCG vaccine.[2]

One is rBCG30, which worked well in animal models. It is a strain of BCG that has been genetically engineered to secrete large amounts of the most abundant protein produced by *Mycobacterium tuberculosis*. This induces a very strong immune response in animals and humans and has been shown to be extremely safe.

Another of these vaccines is rBCGΔureC:Hly. This strain of BCG includes genes from the bacterium *Listeria monocytogenes*. The genes direct the production of an enzyme known as listeriolysin, which helps to sustain an acidic pH in phagosomes. The phagosomal membrane perforates causing increased apoptosis (cell death) and allowing the BCG antigen to enter into the cytoplasm and stimulate cells of the immune system.

Another approach using recombination is aimed at boosting the initial, standard BCG vaccine response. In this method of vaccination, after the initial BCG vaccine is administered, antigens from patients with latent tuberculosis or from those whose disease has been cured are introduced to the individual receiving the vaccine. One example of this uses a genetically engineered virus as a vector to introduce the proteins to the person receiving the vaccine. The virus is no longer virulent, but is able to present the person's immune system with one or more mycobacterial proteins. One drawback is that if the individual has been previously exposed to the natural virus, he or she will have antibodies that will destroy the virus and interfere with the introduction of the bacterial proteins. Another example is to use genetic engineering to create recombinant fusion proteins made of two or three *Mycobacterium tuberculosis* or BCG antigens and inject them into the recipient.

One other technique aimed at creating a vaccine is to use killed whole bacteria to improve the immune response in patients that already have tuberculosis and are being treated with chemotherapy. One approach is to use heat-killed *Mycobacterium vaccae*, a nonpathogenic species of bacteria that naturally lives in soil. The bacteria are introduced into the skin in a multidose series. Clinical trials have shown that there is some improvement in the patients' X-rays and symptomatology, a decrease in time to a negative sputum culture, and an improved cure rate. Another method involves growing *Mycobacterium tuberculosis* in culture under stress conditions and then fragmenting and detoxifying them so that they may be delivered in liposomes (microscopic, artificial sacs made of fatty substances) to the patient.

To combat pulmonary tuberculosis, new ways of delivering the vaccine are being investigated. One study compared the effectiveness of administering BCG vaccine either percutaneously (introduced to the patient by multiple shallow needlesticks into the unbroken skin) or intradermally (injected into the skin in the usual fashion). The conclusion was that the percutaneous route was more efficient in stimulating the immune response.[3]

Another route of administration for vaccines is oral. The polio vaccine has been given orally throughout the world

DID YOU KNOW?

The History of Vaccination: How Cowpox Helped Lead to the Elimination of Smallpox

The term *vaccine* is derived from *vacca*, the Latin word for cow. The practice of preventing disease by inoculation began with variolation, an ancient East Asian custom of exposing oneself to fluid from smallpox lesions to prevent development of a lethal smallpox infection. Centuries later, in 1716, Lady Mary Wortley Montagu, who was the wife of the British ambassador to Turkey, witnessed Turkish women inserting matter from smallpox lesions into the veins of villagers. Following a brief, mild illness the villagers recovered with no smallpox scars. Lady Montagu tried to convince the British Empire to adopt the practice, to no avail. Finally, in 1798, the practice of vaccination became generally accepted thanks to Edward Jenner, an English country doctor. Dr. Jenner learned that milkmaids who contracted cowpox (the bovine form of smallpox and a common consequence of the milking profession) were not susceptible to smallpox. He utilized material from cowpox lesions of milkmaids to vaccinate his patients against smallpox. Smallpox remains the one and only infectious disease eradicated thanks to an effective vaccination program.

successfully since 1960. An Iranian study used BCG encapsulated in alginate microspheres that protected the bacteria from stomach acid and enzymes. Alginate is a naturally occurring substance derived from brown algae. The researchers found that the immune response in mice given the encapsulated BCG was stronger than in mice given the BCG vaccine by injection or orally without being encapsulated.[4]

Delivery of the vaccine via the respiratory route rather than through injection would theoretically provide better protection in the lungs and thus prevent pulmonary infection. A research study designed to determine whether inhaled tuberculosis vaccine would be effective in stimulating a strong immune response to the disease was performed using mice and an adenovirus vector. The recombinant virus was engineered to deliver *Mycobacterium tuberculosis* antigen 85A (Ag85A). The vaccine was introduced into the nasal passages of the mice that were then challenged with live bacteria via the lungs. A strong immune response developed, indicating that this mode of vaccination might be successful.

BCG IS NOT RECOMMENDED
FOR USE IN THE UNITED STATES

BCG is not recommended for use in the United States mainly because tuberculosis rates in the United States are fairly low. In addition, the vaccine induces an immune response in the recipient that may cause a consequential response during Mantoux testing. Following BCG vaccination, interpretation of the screening test would be complicated by the difficulty differentiating a reaction due to actual infection by the bacilli or one caused by the BCG vaccine. This situation is commonly seen in hospitals throughout the United States where many members of the nursing staff are originally from foreign countries such as Haiti, Jamaica, the Dominican Republic, Russia, and other nations where the BCG vaccine is given to newborn babies in all of the hospitals. In the United States, hospitals require employees to get tested annually with a PPD (purified protein derivative) test to ensure that they have not been exposed to tuberculosis while working at the hospital. These vaccinated employees may test positive for tuberculosis even though they have never had the disease. Their immune systems are merely responding to the protein in the injection that stimulates the immune reaction based on the original vaccine. The benefits of BCG vaccination may also be outweighed by the fact that the risk for tuberculosis is relatively low in the United States compared to other parts of the world.

In lieu of vaccination, U.S. public health officials have developed a three-part strategy to combat the disease. The strategy includes the following points: 1) early detection and treatment; 2) antibiotic therapy for people who are infected but do not have clinical disease; and 3) prevention of institutional (prisons, hospitals) transmission with effective tuberculosis control programs.

Although not recommended for routine use, there are some situations in which the vaccine may be administered in the United States. People who qualify for vaccination fall into the following groups:

- Children who are continuously exposed to an untreated person with infectious pulmonary tuberculosis if the child cannot be removed from the home

- Children who are continuously exposed to someone with **multiple drug-resistant tuberculosis (MDR-TB)** if they cannot be removed from the home

- Health-care workers in a setting with a large number of MDR-TB individuals and where conventional tuberculosis control programs have not been successful

BCG is not recommended in the following instances:

- For adults or children with **HIV (human immuno-deficiency virus)**, as well as other immunocompromised individuals

- As a requirement for employment of health-care workers

- For pregnant women

- For health-care workers in settings where the risk of transmission is low.

9

Treatment of Tuberculosis I: Sanatoriums and Early Drug Treatments

Gregory was a railroad worker in New York in the late 1800s. He put in long, hard hours at his job and was a good family man. He wanted his family to have what they needed for a comfortable life, so he got little rest and worked as much as possible to earn a wage that would make life easier on the rest of his family.

Gregory's many hours of work and few hours of sleep contributed to his being very tired much of the time. Nevertheless, he kept working. Unfortunately, his life wore down his body to the point where he was easily infected by tuberculosis bacteria when he was exposed to the disease by his close contact with another railroad worker whom he saw every day for months.

There was no medical treatment for tuberculosis at this time, and Gregory was afraid that he might spread the disease to the rest of his family. However, because he lived in New York, his doctor suggested that he travel to Saranac Lake, in upstate New York, where a sanatorium had been opened specifically for patients with tuberculosis. Perhaps the cold air, a healthy lifestyle, and lots of rest would be the key to his recovery.

In the past few decades, tuberculosis has reemerged, causing more than 2 million deaths annually. The emergence of AIDS has contributed to the increased case rate of tuberculosis in industrialized countries. AIDS, civil wars, weakened economies, and the lack of public health programs have all increased the rates of tuberculosis in less developed countries. What makes the incidence of this disease so shocking is that the increase in tuberculosis cases comes at a time when effective antimicrobial treatments are available to treat the disease and kill the organism. These effective treatments were not always available. In the past, cures, concoctions, and approaches to treating tuberculosis have been varied, and the results were often deadly.

EARLY TREATMENTS

In ancient times, most disease was thought to be due to an imbalance of body humors (body fluids believed to be responsible for one's personality and health). The humors included black bile, yellow bile, phlegm, and blood. To regain the balance, bloodletting was a classical treatment. From the era of Hippocrates through the 20th century, bleeding of the patient was an accepted, if not particularly effective, therapeutic approach to treating tuberculosis. The combination of bloodletting with the hemorrhaging that sometimes occurred in the lungs surely sent many patients to their deaths prematurely.

Since tuberculosis was considered a wasting disease, a common therapy was to provide a nutritious diet. Both Galen and Hippocrates recommended the consumption of milk, and advocated avoidance of meat and alcohol, both thought to cause a major imbalance of the humors. Hippocrates defined the diet even further by suggesting that the patient should avoid beef, but properly cooked pork was permitted and could promote healing. The diet recommendations of Galen and Hippocrates were followed through the 1800s. In addition, sweet elixirs for cough supplemented with opia camphorate (opium) were recommended.

As the science of chemistry developed in the 1800s, several chemical cures or treatments were used for tuberculosis. Chloride

> ### DID YOU KNOW?
>
> Creosote is an oily liquid derived from either wood tar or coal tar. Creosote is often used to coat railroad ties or landscaping timbers to protect the wood from the elements. The active antimicrobial compound in creosote is cresol, a phenolic (containing phenol) compound. Phenols have both antibacterial and antiviral properties and are often used as disinfectants.

of sodium, chloride of lime, chlorine gas, digitalis, hydrocyanic acid, iodine, and creosote were among the compounds used to treat tuberculosis. The value of these remedies is debatable, and their use may have hastened the death of more than a few tuberculosis patients. However, it is interesting to note that a synthesized form of creosote, guaifenesin, can still be found today in cough drops or cough syrups used to quiet a chronic cough. It is classifed as an expectorant and acts by thinning mucus in the air passages.

Perhaps one of the most unusual attempts to cure tuberculosis took place in Mammoth Cave, Kentucky. In 1839, Mammoth Cave was purchased by a Louisville physician, Dr. John Croghan. Dr. Croghan was particularly interested in the healing properties of the caves. He believed the cave's constant temperature and humidity might help those suffering from tuberculosis.

Dr. Croghan admitted patients to wood and stone dwellings that had been constructed along the central trails in the cave in the spring of 1842. Legend has it that if one visited the caves at this time, he or she would be greeted by the sight of pale, emaciated individuals inside the huts and the sounds of constant coughing. Unfortunately, the cool temperatures and high humidity seemed to make the patients worse and several died (moist climate fosters transmission of the disease). The experiment ended in failure, and those who survived were taken out of the caves.

Dr. Croghan himself died of tuberculosis in 1849. Today, one can visit the caves and still see two stone huts that remain from the failed experiment.

THE SANATORIUM MOVEMENT

The industrial age brought with it large, crowded cities that were often smelly and filthy. Open sewers and poor sanitation made the air unfavorable to the healing of a lung disease such as tuberculosis. Mild climates with clear mountain or salt air and pine forests were the direct opposite of city living and were often recommended as a cure. The search for treatment in a favorable climate gave rise to the construction of **sanatoriums** for the treatment of tuberculosis.

In 1854, Hermann Brehmer founded one of the first sanatoriums, in the Bavarian Alps of Germany. The complex had 40 rooms, several common entertainment rooms, and a kitchen. The sanatorium was located in a mountain valley approximately 1,715 feet above sea level.

Brehmer believed that the small, weak hearts of tuberculosis patients (which he had seen as a medical student, studying the anatomy of cadavers) could be compensated for by living above sea level. This would allow the metabolism of the patients to improve and permit the body to heal itself of the offending disease, tuberculosis. Brehmer was encouraged in his assumptions by a German explorer who wrongly insisted that tuberculosis did not exist in populations who lived in mountainous regions.

Brehmer's sanatorium routine consisted of moderate exercise followed by rest, consumption of a nutritious diet, and the drinking of fresh spring water. By 1904, his sanatorium was the largest in the world and was able to accommodate 300 patients at a time. Dr. Brehmer's sanatorium, both in design and approach, soon came to be imitated all over Europe and in the United States.

The mountain resorts of Switzerland, particularly the village of Davos, were very popular with the wealthier victims of tuberculosis. This type of sanatorium, which featured elegant

Figure 9.1 Edward Livingston Trudeau, pictured above, suffered from tuberculosis before moving to the Adirondack mountains in 1873. During his time there, his health improved, and he believed that the mountain air would do that same for others suffering from the disease. Dr. Trudeau opened a sanatorium on Saranac Lake, the first tuberculosis sanatorium in the United States. When he was not treating tuberculosis patients, he conducted experiments with the tubercle bacillus. (Courtesy of the Adirondack Museum)

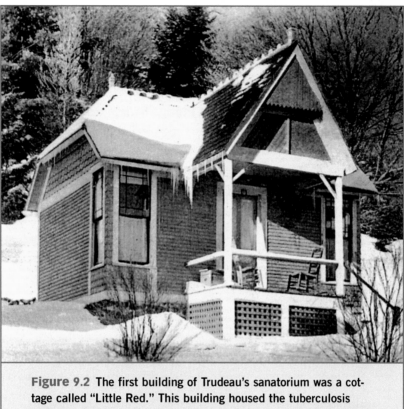

Figure 9.2 The first building of Trudeau's sanatorium was a cottage called "Little Red." This building housed the tuberculosis patients who hoped that the clean mountain air would rid them of their tuberculosis. Little Red, pictured here, and Trudeau's sanatorium started a large sanatorium movement in the United States. Within 50 years, the United States had over 600 such facilities. (Courtesy of the Adirondack Museum)

rooms, lavish meals, and minimal medical treatment, was the setting for the famous book by Thomas Mann called *The Magic Mountain*. In Mann's story the hero, Hans Castorp, spends seven years recovering from tuberculosis only to bid readers farewell as he runs through cannon fire in World War I.

The American sanatorium movement began with Edward Livingston Trudeau, who went to the Adirondacks in 1873, two years after his graduation from medical school, expecting to die from tuberculosis. He was very familiar with the disease after having taken care of his brother who was diagnosed and died of tuberculosis in a short, four-month period. Trudeau expected the same fate. However, while in the Adirondacks his health improved. He moved back to New York City, became ill, and then improved again upon moving back to Saranac Lake (118 miles north of Albany, New York).

With financial help from his friends and other generous donors, Trudeau purchased some land in Saranac Lake and began construction of a cottage on the property. The cottage, "Little Red," would provide housing for tuberculosis patients who would, hopefully, improve as Trudeau had.

In 1885, Trudeau admitted two patients to the cottages he had constructed. He also set up a laboratory on the grounds. After reading a translation of Koch's work on the infectious nature of tuberculosis, he managed to grow the tubercle bacillus, repeat Koch's experiments, and even test for the organism in samples from his patients' sputum. The Saranac Lake laboratory was the first in the United States to study tuberculosis. From its simple beginnings, the Trudeau Institute at Saranac Lake went on to train ex–patients to be nurses and provide post-graduate education at the Trudeau School for Tuberculosis, established in 1916.

Trudeau died of his tuberculosis in 1916 at the age of 68. Although he did not see many cures, he did start a movement. By 1904, there were 115 sanatoriums in the United States; by 1923, 656 facilities; and by 1953, 839 facilities that could care for 130,322 tuberculosis patients.

Sanatoriums also had a hand in changing personal habits and fashions. Men were encouraged to shave their beards and trim mustaches so as not to trap sputum from their coughs. Consumptive women were advised to shorten their hair, wear lighter dresses, and raise their hems above ankle level to avoid gathering dust, which might be contaminated with tubercle bacilli.

Figure 9.3 Following the opening of Dr. Trudeau's Saranac Lake sanatorium, many other such treatment centers quickly sprang up all over the country. Patients were encouraged to sleep outdoors, even in the cold weather, where fresh air would, it was hoped, lead to their cure. (© Bettmann/Corbis)

DID YOU KNOW?

George Orwell, born Eric Blair, a famous British author who wrote the books *Animal Farm* and *Nineteen Eighty-Four*, began his war with tuberculosis in 1938. While spending time in a sanatorium in 1947, he was able to secure a shipment of streptomycin from the United States. At first the antibiotic helped Orwell, but then side effects started to appear. In Orwell's own words, "A sort of discoloration appeared at the base of my fingers and toenails; then my face became red and the skin began to flake off and a rash appeared all over my body, especially down my back . . . meanwhile my nails had disintegrated and my hair began to fall out in patches. It was very unpleasant." Not able to tolerate streptomycin treatment, Orwell died of tuberculosis in 1948. He was 46 years old.

Source: B. Crick, *George Orwell: A Life* (London: Penguin, 1992), p. 560.

Some patients liked the sheltered, structured environment of the sanatorium; others considered it confining and isolating. The system did enable physicians to observe the disease in a controlled environment, and the isolation of patients in sanatoriums may have helped prevent transmission.

The incidence of tuberculosis declined during the period of sanatorium treatment, although this was probably due to many factors. Much medical advancement also occurred during this period. *Mycobacterium tuberculosis* was discovered as the causative agent, X-rays were discovered, and tuberculin, originally described by Koch as a tuberculosis cure, provided a means to diagnose infection with the organism.

THE ANTIBIOTIC ERA

The antibiotic era of tuberculosis treatment began in 1946 with the discovery and use of streptomycin to treat tuberculosis.

Prior to the use of antibiotics, approximately 50% of patients with lung disease died. With the use of antibiotics, the mortality rate dropped to less than 10%.

Although streptomycin resulted in successful treatment for some patients, in others the antibiotic failed to produce improvement. Some patients had severe allergic reactions to the drug, and in others antibiotic-resistant tubercle bacilli began to emerge.

To avoid the problem of antibiotic resistance, it was found to be advantageous to use two or more drugs in combination. This method proved to be successful because it was more difficult for mutant organisms to arise spontaneously through genetic change to more than one drug.

The combination of para-aminosalicylic acid (PAS) and streptomycin worked better than streptomycin alone. Isoniazid (first synthesized in 1912 and found to be effective against tuberculosis in 1951) and pyrazinamide were introduced in 1952 and proved almost 100 percent effective for tuberculosis patients. Both drugs had to be taken by the patient for almost a year and a half. This caused some problems with compliance because the drugs were expensive (it cost $3,500 to treat one patient with streptomycin and PAS) and on occasion produced side effects.

Rifampin was first made available in 1967. The combination of rifampin and isoniazid allowed the treatment time to be reduced from 18 to 6 months.

10

Treatment of Tuberculosis II: Modern Drug Therapy

In the early 1990s, a man was infected with multiple drug-resistant tuberculosis (MDR-TB) in New York. Undiagnosed, he moved to South Carolina where he infected three family members and a neighbor. One of his family members later underwent a bronchoscopy, a procedure used to examine the airway branches that connect to the lungs. A bronchoscope is the name of the device inserted into the windpipe to view the airways and lung tissue.

That same unsterilized bronchoscope was then used to examine six other people, five of whom eventually died from tuberculosis. The strain of tuberculosis that killed the five was designated the "W" strain. This strain arose in New York City in 1990 and is resistant to seven different drugs. Death rates from infection with the W strain can exceed 80 %.

The above story illustrates the need to prevent development of MDR-TB as well as the need for quick diagnosis and appropriate treatment of active cases of tuberculosis.

DRUG THERAPY

For the majority of patients, tuberculosis treatment includes an initial two-month course of therapy with four anti-tuberculosis drugs: isoniazid, rifampin, pyrazinamide, and ethambutol. This treatment is then followed by four months of isoniazid and rifampin only.

Ideally, the acid-fast bacillus should be isolated from the patient's sputum. This isolate should then be tested for drug susceptibility to determine the most optimal course of antibiotic therapy. Unfortunately, because of slow bacterial growth, it takes at least three weeks to test for drug susceptibility.

Because time is of the essence, it is best to begin treatment with the four drugs before drug susceptibility is determined. Treatment can then be modified based upon susceptibility tests. In the case where the chance of drug resistance of the isolate is low, three drugs may be adequate for treatment. However, at least two drugs must always be used to treat tuberculosis disease in order to prevent the emergence of drug resistant bacilli.

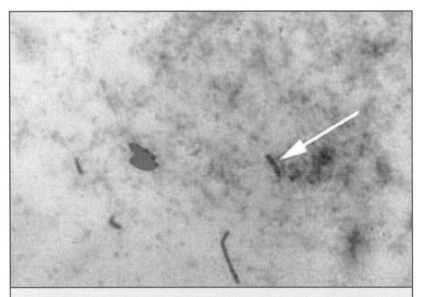

Figure 10.1 Tuberculosis bacilli can be identified in a sputum sample using the acid-fast stain. Bacteria that are classified as acid-fast can retain a primary stain when washed with alcohol. These cells have a waxy cell wall that prevents acidic alcohol from removing the initial stain. In the picture above, *Mycobacterium tuberculosis* cells, which are acid-fast, appear pink. (Centers for Disease Control and Prevention)

Some patients with tuberculosis infection, not disease, may be prescribed medication because of other risk factors. In this situation, a single drug, isoniazid, is prescribed for six to 12 months.

WHY DOES DRUG RESISTANCE DEVELOP?

A bacterial strain is considered drug resistant if the frequency of drug-resistant organisms in the bacterial population is 1% or greater. Initially, in drug-sensitive tuberculosis infections, one in 1 million bacilli is naturally resistant to isoniazid, and one in 100 million bacilli is resistant to rifampin. When a patient is treated with one antibiotic, the drug-resistant strain will continue to replicate and eventually outnumber the drug-sensitive organisms. In a short time, a frequency of 1% drug-resistant organisms can easily be obtained in the large bacterial populations found in active tuberculosis disease.

Mycobacterium tuberculosis resistance to rifampicin may develop due to genetic changes that bring about an alteration in the affinity to the antibiotic or decreased permeability of the cell wall. Other mutations may affect the bacterium's ribosomal susceptibility to streptomycin, making the bacterium resistant to the antibiotic's ability to block protein synthesis. Yet another mutation may change the gene responsible for ethambutol's

DID YOU KNOW?

The tubercle bacilli become resistant to isoniazid in an unusual way. Instead of actively acquiring resistance, the organism loses its susceptibility to the drug. This happens when the bacilli loses the gene that encodes the enzyme that renders the bacterium vulnerable to the drug. This is possible because isoniazid has no antibacterial activity itself but requires the bacteria to produce an enzyme to convert the drug to an active antimicrobial form.

ability to interfere with cell wall production in *Mycobacterium tuberculosis*, leading to the normal development of the wall and resistance to the antibiotic.

If two drugs are used to treat tuberculosis, the expected frequency of bacterial mutation to resistance to both drugs is one organism in a population of approximately 10^{14} to 10^{20}. Because this frequency is so low, drug resistance is less likely to develop when more than two drugs are prescribed.

Multiple drug-resistant tuberculosis (MDR-TB) is defined as resistance to two or more tuberculosis drugs. Drug resistance may emerge naturally at the rates described above. However, it

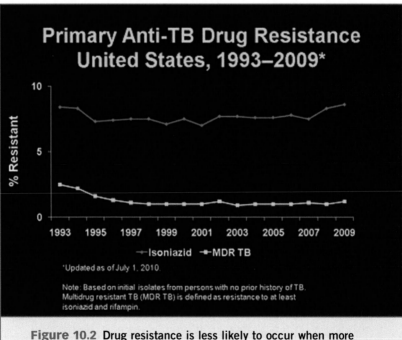

Figure 10.2 Drug resistance is less likely to occur when more than one drug is used to treat tuberculosis. In the United States, approximately 7 to 8.6% of *Mycobacterium tuberculosis* isolates are found to be resistant to isoniazid, while less than 2% of all isolates are found to be resistant to two or more tuberculosis drugs. (Centers for Disease Control and Prevention)

is more likely to emerge as a treatment problem due to insufficient therapy, inappropriate therapy, and the failure of the patient to comply with prescribed therapy. Malabsorption of medications due to malnourishment may also contribute to the emergence of drug resistance.

PREVENTING THE EMERGENCE OF MULTIPLE DRUG RESISTANCE

Treating someone with MDR-TB may cost up to $250,000 and take more than two years. It is therefore imperative that initial treatment be continued for the appropriate period of time to prevent the emergence of drug-resistant organisms. The patient must take all drugs as prescribed and not stop when he or she is feeling better. Patients often discontinue medication because of common side effects such as diarrhea and nausea. Unfortunately, stopping medication too soon will give rise to multiple-antibiotic-resistant organisms.

DIRECTLY OBSERVED THERAPY (DOT)

It is estimated that 20% of all tuberculosis patients fail to complete drug therapy. To insure that patients take their drugs as prescribed, **directly observed therapy** or DOT is employed. In DOT, a caregiver insures that the patient is taking drugs by observing use directly. This approach is very expensive, and can tax public health resources. On the other hand, DOT is extremely effective at eliminating disease and preventing the evolution of MDR-TB.

DOT therapy was instituted successfully in New York City to eliminate the tuberculosis that raged through Harlem in the early 1990s. A few years ago, an immigrant neighborhood in Queens called Corona utilized the same approach to quash a tuberculosis outbreak. In Corona, health care workers observed 10 to 15 patients a day, five days a week, taking their medication. Patients who complied were rewarded with fast food coupons or food items.

Sometimes it is necessary to implement DOT under confined conditions. In New York City, the modern-day version of the sanatorium has returned. Patients who fail to take their medication may be held against their will, confined to a tuberculosis ward in a hospital.

Coler-Goldwater Specialty Hospital in New York City is a facility where city health officials can detain tuberculosis patients for months until they are cured. Patients are not allowed out of the tuberculosis ward during the term of treatment. They sleep in private or four-patient rooms complete with televisions and telephones. Other amenities include a recreation room with billiards, drug treatment and psychiatric counseling, and educational tutoring.

Most patients complain that forced confinement to a tuberculosis treatment facility takes away their civil liberties. City health officials attempt to balance public health with private freedoms. Before patients are confined, they are provided with a lawyer paid for by the city and have the right to fight in court against confinement.

Regardless of how it is applied, DOT cures disease, prevents transmission, and prevents the development of multiple drug resistance. Although DOT is proven successful, the World Health Organization reports that DOT has been slow to be fully implemented worldwide due in part to its cost and the requirement for a (government) public health infrastructure in the countries affected.

TREATMENT OF DRUG-RESISTANT TUBERCULOSIS

Patients who have drug-resistant tuberculosis may be required to take more than 20 pills per day for a period of up to two years. The drugs employed will be "second-line" drugs, which are usually not as effective as the first-choice drugs. Second-line drugs usually cause more side effects and are more toxic to the host.

Second-line drugs include ciprofloxacin, sparifloxacin, ofloxacin, clarithromycin, thionamides, macrolides, clofazimine, and amoxicillin plus clavulanic acid. Side effects from these drugs include kidney toxicity, neurotoxicity, severe gastrointestinal upset, skin problems, and liver toxicity. In addition to utilizing second-line drugs to treat MDR-TB, surgery to remove infected tissue may be considered.

THE SEARCH FOR NEW DRUGS

Because drug resistance continues to emerge, it is necessary to search for and develop new anti-mycobacterial medications. Sequencing of the tuberculosis genome has provided new information about the organism. Sequence information and the elucidation of gene function will provide information to develop new drugs. Of particular interest is the development of drugs that remain in the body longer. More stable drugs require fewer doses and shorter therapy. It is also important to develop drugs that do not interfere with anti-HIV medications since the HIV-positive population of individuals has greatly affected the incidence of tuberculosis.

When treating tuberculosis with medication, it is important to remember that there may be two different populations of tubercle bacilli in the body: the rapidly growing organisms, which are easily and quickly killed by medication, and the more slowly replicating (or perhaps not growing at all) population of bacilli, which require an extended course of drug therapy.

A group of researchers looking for new drug targets is focusing on the ability of the bacterium to exist inside the host cell for many years (latency). By studying the metabolism of the bacteria, scientists have learned that rather than yielding carbon from the breakdown of sugars in a biological pathway called the Krebs cycle, mycobacteria inside the tubercle obtain carbon from fats via a pathway called the glyoxylate shunt. To harvest the carbon, the organisms use an enzyme called isocitrate lyase. This enzyme is produced only in some animals, plants, and bacteria; it is not found in humans. Turning off this enzyme with a drug would starve the bacteria inside the tuberculosis lesion, resulting in a complete cure. Destruction of this molecular target would not cause side effects in the human host because the enzyme does not exist in host cells.

In addition to searching for new drug targets, pharmaceutical companies are also tinkering with currently used drugs to make them more effective. Rifabutin and rifapentine are derivatives of rifamycin, which may be used instead of rifampin. Rifabutin appears to be more active against *Mycobacterium tuberculosis* than rifamycin (rifampin), without being more toxic to the host.

11

The Human Immunodeficiency Virus and Tuberculosis

Marcus was diagnosed with HIV three years ago. He has been receiving HAART (highly active antiretroviral therapy) treatment for the viral infection. The progress of the infection has been slowed down by the treatment, but his immune system is still quite compromised.

One day about six months ago he was visiting his girlfriend Jill, who also has HIV. He was very happy to see her and they kissed. Right after this she mentioned in conversation that she most likely was exposed to someone with tuberculosis. He didn't think anything of it at the time and continued to kiss and hug his girlfriend. Jill coughed several times during the visit, but she seemed otherwise fine.

It turned out that Jill was indeed exposed to a person with an active case of tuberculosis, and she contracted it. Because of Marcus's weakened immune system, he, too, contracted tuberculosis. When he and Jill were tested for bacterial susceptibility to antibiotics, it turned out that they were both infected with MDR tuberculosis. That is, their strain of Mycobacterium tuberculosis *is resistant to both rifampin and isoniazid. This is very common in patients who have both HIV infection and tuberculosis. Unfortunately, this makes treating the bacterial infection much more difficult.*

Another problem that both Jill and Marcus face is the possible interaction of the drugs used to treat both diseases. Immune reconstitution inflammatory syndrome (IRIS), an overreaction of the immune system that allows the tuberculosis to become worse, may occur in patients receiving medication for both conditions. Their doctors must be extremely careful when treating Jill and Marcus. Careful balancing between the medications will be a constant challenge.

Five cases of a new life-threatening disease were first reported in Los Angeles in 1981. Patients appeared to have a bad case of influenza. Instead of recovering from their initial illness, the patients began dying from rare complications. These complications included a fungal lung infection caused by *Pneumocystis carinii* and a cancer of the skin called Kaposi's sarcoma. The rare complications of the initial disease suggested that the patient's immune system was functioning poorly, if at all. The disease was given the name acquired immune deficiency syndrome, or AIDS, to reflect the fact that infected individuals had very impaired immune systems.

In 1983, French researchers at the Pasteur Institute provided evidence that AIDS was caused by a retrovirus. The virus, originally called LAV (lymphadenopathy virus), was designated HIV (human immunodeficiency virus) in 1986.

AIDS patients have a sharp decrease in their population of T lymphocytes. These T lymphocytes are responsible for releasing lymphokines which recruit and activate macrophage and cytotoxic cells. Lymphokines are very important in the specific immune response that prevents tuberculosis infection from ultimately developing into tuberculosis disease. HIV can also infect macrophages, other critical cells in the war against tuberculosis disease.

AIDS AND TUBERCULOSIS—DEADLY PARTNERS

The association between HIV and tuberculosis first became apparent in 1987 when diagnosis of disseminated tuberculosis became part of the case definition of AIDS. Tuberculosis is now considered the most common cause of death in persons with HIV infection.

In individuals who are HIV positive, the mortality rate from MDR-TB is between 70 and 90%, with most patients

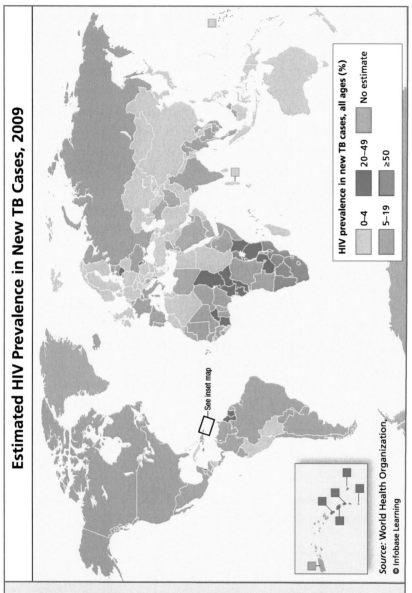

Figure 11.1 Africa has the highest reports of people infected with both HIV and tuberculosis. The southern tip of the African continent alone has over 50% HIV prevalence in new tuberculosis cases. The map pictured above, courtesy of the World Health Organization's Global Tuberculosis Control Report for 2010, details different incidence rates in each country throughout the world.

succumbing to tuberculosis in an average of four months. To complicate matters further, 90% of all MDR-TB occurs in HIV positive individuals.

HIV infection promotes progression of tuberculosis infection to tuberculosis disease, and tuberculosis disease may accelerate HIV replication. Persons with AIDS (see box on page 110 for a discussion of HIV and AIDS) have rapidly progressing, newly acquired tuberculosis infection, and because of the detrimental effects of HIV on T lymphocytes, reactivation of latent tuberculosis is very likely.

The World Health Organization reports that in 2008 nearly 11 million people worldwide were infected with both tuberculosis and HIV. Approximately three-fourths of them live in Africa. HIV has been blamed for a fourfold rise in the incidence of tuberculosis, particularly in the sub-Saharan region of the continent. In addition, of the estimated 1.7 million people who died of tuberculosis in 2007, 24% were also infected with HIV.

DIAGNOSIS OF TUBERCULOSIS
IN HIV-POSITIVE INDIVIDUALS

In 1991, at a San Francisco residence for HIV-positive individuals, 12 of 31 residents became infected with tuberculosis during a five-month period. Genetic evaluation of the infecting *Mycobacterium tuberculosis* strain showed that one resident had infected the rest. This scenario demonstrates how quickly the tubercle bacilli can spread through a susceptible population.

Unfortunately, diagnosis of tuberculosis in HIV-positive individuals may be difficult. Approximately 50% of those infected do not respond to the Mantoux test because of weakened immune systems. In those who do respond to testing, the size of the zone of induration may be smaller than expected: 5 mm or less. Length of HIV infection will determine the testing response, as those who are more recently diagnosed as HIV positive will produce a larger area of induration in the Mantoux test than those who have been infected with HIV for an extended period of time. People who have been infected with

WHAT IS THE DIFFERENCE BETWEEN SOMEONE WHO IS HIV POSITIVE AND SOMEONE WHO HAS AIDS?

An HIV-positive individual, or someone who is infected with HIV, has had the virus enter the body and begin replicating. As HIV infection progresses, the virus continues to replicate and begins causing damage to the body, particularly the immune system. Strictly speaking, AIDS is the term used to describe the end stage of HIV infection. AIDS is characterized by immune deficiency, the development of tumors, and the occurrence of opportunistic infections. Without treatment, almost everyone who is infected with HIV ultimately progresses to having AIDS and finally death.

HIV for many years are least likely to respond to a Mantoux test even though they may have active tuberculosis. Diagnosis of tuberculosis may further be complicated because of the difficulty encountered when attempting to culture tubercle bacilli from AIDS patients.

Because people with AIDS do not always respond to tuberculosis tests, there may be a delay in correctly diagnosing tuberculosis in these individuals. During this time, the patient can transmit tuberculosis unknowingly.

CLINICAL FEATURES OF HIV-POSITIVE INDIVIDUALS

The clinical features of tuberculosis infection will depend upon the health of the immune system of the HIV-positive patient. Those infected with tuberculosis early during HIV progression have more typical tuberculosis disease, with the upper portions of the lungs most often infected. As HIV infection progresses, tubercles usually develop more deeply in the lungs. Also in advanced HIV infection, or AIDS, tuberculosis will more likely be disseminated, often resulting in inflammation of the membrane covering the heart (pericarditis), the lining of the abdomen (peritonitis), or the lining covering the brain and spinal cord (meningitis). The tubercle bacilli may also spread to bones and joints.

Expected X-ray findings such as spots related to calcified tubercles are seen in 50 percent or less of infected AIDS patients. Diagnosis is further complicated because pulmonary tuberculosis is easily confused with other opportunistic lung infections, Kaposi's sarcoma, or lymphoma.

TREATMENT

Because the course of tuberculosis may be greatly accelerated in AIDS patients, treatment usually begins as soon as tuberculosis is suspected. HIV-positive individuals often fail to respond to the Mantoux test; therefore, preventive therapy should be prescribed even when the tuberculosis test is negative. Preventive isoniazid is prescribed for 12 months to HIV-positive patients exposed to someone who has tuberculosis. For those in whom tuberculosis has been diagnosed, the normal four-drug regimen is prescribed for a period of nine months (rather than six).

Patients with known tuberculosis and AIDS should begin treatment in a separate environment for at least the first two weeks of therapy. Isolation should include housing in a separate room with a closed door and adequate ventilation. Air from the room should be exhausted to the outside of the building. Bactericidal ultraviolet light and air filtration should be used as a further precaution. Health-care workers coming in contact with the HIV/tuberculosis patient should wear a respirator and be periodically tested for tuberculosis.

Directly observed therapy (DOT) is an absolute requirement for intravenous drug users and homeless persons who have AIDS and tuberculosis. Special precautions regarding isolation must be taken in health care settings when HIV-positive individuals are treated. MDR-TB is especially prevalent in this environment.

AIDS patients often take five to ten medications to treat their disease. Selected anti-tuberculosis medication should not interact with the prescribed medications. Of particular concern is the interaction of protease inhibitors used to treat AIDS with rifampin. Protease inhibitors combined with rifampin have been shown to increase rifampin's toxicity. For IV drug users in treatment receiving methadone, special caution must be used because methadone can interact with rifampin.

The BCG vaccine should not be administered to HIV-positive patients in whom it can cause disease in the spine, cardiovascular system, or brain.

ECONOMIC AND ETHICAL CONCERNS

In the New York Criminal Courts Building in Brooklyn, more than 200 criminal suspects are herded into holding pens each day. Each 10 x 15 foot pen holds 12 or more detainees who stay two to three days. Many of the suspects are homeless, are intra-venous drug users, or have AIDS, while some fall into all of the previously mentioned categories. Thousands pass through these unventilated holding pens each month. Corrections officers are afraid, lawyers are afraid, and even the inmates are afraid of catching a dreaded disease like tuberculosis in this environment.

Prisons, HIV, and tuberculosis are a deadly combination. Prisoners are housed in large groups, eating, living, and work-ing together. Older prison buildings have poor ventilation. More than 80% of prisoners have used street drugs and approx-imately 65% of prison inmates have AIDS and tuberculosis. All of these conditions and factors combine to promote the trans-mission of tuberculosis in prisons.

Unfortunately, states have little money to provide appropri-ate isolation and treatment for infected inmates, although some states, New York in particular, have attempted to provide isola-tion wards to treat infected prisoners.

Homeless people who are HIV positive and have tuberculosis are of particular concern to public health workers. Once released from prison, these individuals need access to housing. Unfortunately, local governments may experience difficulty in providing housing in a supervised environment before these inmates are released from prison or discharged from the hospital.

In states where HIV infection is common, only AIDS cases are reportable. There is no mandated treatment or confinement of the sexually active HIV-positive individual who may be infecting others. Tuberculosis control laws, on the other hand, include mandated testing, treatment, and, if needed, confinement. These differences may be due to the fact that tuberculosis can be spread by casual contact (coughing) and also because the disease poses a serious public health threat. This threat requires patient identification, isolation, treatment, and contact information. Knowledge of a patient's HIV status is essential to ensure proper tuberculosis care. Balancing patient confidentiality regarding HIV and tuberculosis risk and infection will continue to be a challenge for public–health care workers.

WHAT'S NEXT?

It is clear that HIV/AIDS and tuberculosis is a global problem; so it will take a global effort to develop resources and strategies to eliminate both diseases.

In 1989, public health service support in the United States for tuberculosis research totaled less than $5 million. By 1999 that figure was approximately $70 million (according to the National Institutes of Health and the Centers for Disease Control and Prevention). Now, with the passage of the Comprehensive TB Elimination Act of 2008 (HR 1532), the United States Government has authorized $200,000,000 for fiscal year 2009, $210,000,000 for fiscal year 2010, $220,500,000 for fiscal year 2011, $231,525,000 for fiscal year 2012, and $243,101,250 for fiscal year 2013 to fund tuberculosis programs managed by the Centers for Disease Control and Prevention.

The annual cost of tuberculosis worldwide is estimated to be $4 billion. Clearly, worldwide efforts aimed at treating and preventing the disease will be worth the cost. Regarding the HIV/tuberculosis partnership, says Dr. Peter Piot, executive director of the Joint United Nations Programme on HIV-AIDS, "effectively treating tuberculosis will not solve the worldwide AIDS crisis but it will significantly reduce its burden."[1]

Chapter 1

1. Barron Lerner, "Charting the Death of Eleanor Roosevelt," Fathom Knowledge Network—Columbia University, http://www.fathom.com/feature/35672/index.html (accessed January 6, 2011).

Chapter 2

1. D. S. Burke, "Of Postulates and Peccadilloes: Robert Koch and Vaccine (Tuberculin) Therapy for Tuberculosis," *Vaccine* 11 (1993): 795–804.

Chapter 4

1. Vinay Kumar, et al., *Robbins Basic Pathology*, 8th ed. (Philadelphia: Saunders Elsevier, 2007), 516–522.
2. Centers for Disease Control and Prevention, "Cover Your Cough," http://www.cdc.gov/flu/protect/covercough.htm (accessed December 7, 2010).

Chapter 5

1. Thierry Garnier, et al., "The Complete Genome Sequence of *Mycobacterium bovis*," *Proceedings of the National Academy of Sciences* 100, no. 13 (June 3, 2003), http://www.pnas.org/content/100/13/7877.full (accessed December 9, 2010).
2. Elizabeth A. Talbot, M.D., "*Mycobacterium bovis*," UpToDate, September 1, 2009, http://www.uptodate.com/patients/content/topic.o?topicKey=~Ub3HkGaywSm9y5H (accessed December 9, 2010).
3. Rita M. Washko et al., "*Mycobacterium tuberculosis* Infection in a Green-Winged Macaw (*Ara chloroptera*): Report with Public Health Implications," *Journal of Clinical Microbiology* 36, no. 4 (April 1998), 1101–1102, http://www.ncbi.nlm.nih.gov/pmc/articles/PMC104697 (accessed December 12, 2010).
4. Sir David King, "Bovine Tuberculosis in Cattle and Badgers," *Report to the Secretary of State About Tuberculosis in Cattle and Badgers,* July 30, 2007, http://www.bis.gov.uk/assets/biscore/corporate/migratedD/ec_group/44-07-S_I_on (accessed December 13, 2010).

5. John H. Kirk, D.V.M., "Tuberculosis in Cattle," School of Veterinary Medicine, University of California Davis, May 16, 2002, http://www.vetmed.ucdavis.edu/vetext/INF-DA/Tuberculosis.pdf (accessed December 13, 2010).

Chapter 6

1. Omar H. Vandal, Carl F. Nathan, and Sabine Ehrt, "Acid Resistance in *Mycobacterium tuberculosis*," *Journal of Bacteriology* 191, no. 15 (August 2009): 4714–4721, http://jb.asm.org/cgi/reprint/191/15/4714 (accessed December 14, 2010).

Chapter 7

1. Catharina C. Boehme, M.D., et al., "Rapid Molecular Detection of Tuberculosis and Rifampin Resistance," *New England Journal of Medicine* 363 (September 9, 2010): 1005–1015, http://www.nejm.org/doi/full/10.1056/NEJMoa0907847 (accessed January 6, 2011).
2. J. M. Grange, "Environmental mycobacteria," in *Medical Microbiology,* 17th ed. (Burlington, Mass.: Elsevier Publishers, 2007), 221–227.
3. David E. Griffith et al., "American Thoracic Society Guidelines: Diagnosis, Treatment and Prevention of Nontuberculous Mycobacterial Diseases," *American Journal of Respiratory and Critical Care Medicine,* 175 (2007): 367–417.
4. M. A. DeGroote and G. Huitt, "Infections Due to Rapidly Growing Mycobacteria," *Clinical Infectious Diseases* 42 (2006): 1756–1763.

Chapter 8

1. Vanderbilt University Medical Center, "TB Vaccine Gets Its Groove Back," Science-Daily, May 24, 2009, http://www.sciencedaily.com/releases/2009/05/090519152446.htm (accessed January 3, 2011).
2. Stefan Kaufmann, Gregory Hussey, and Paul-Henri Lambert, "New Vaccines for Tuberculosis," *Lancet* 375, no. 9731 (May 19, 2010): 2110–2119, http://www.thelancet.com/journals/lancet/article/

PIIS0140–6736%2810%2960393–5/full-text (accessed January 3, 2011).

3. V. Davids, et al., "The Effect of Bacille Calmette-Guérin Vaccine Strain and Route of Administration on Induced Immune Responses in Vaccinated Infants," *The Journal of Infectious Diseases* 193, no. 4 (February 15, 2006): 531–536.

4. Soheila Ajdari, et al., "Oral Administration of BCG Encapsulated in Alginate Microspheres Induces Strong Th1 Response in BALB/c Mice," *Vaccine* 25, no. 23 (June 6, 2007): 4595–4601.

Chapter 11

1. Dr. Peter Piot, Executive Director of the Joint United Nations Programme on HIV-AIDS (UNAIDS) in *Stop TB News*, Issue 4, Summer 2001.

acid-fast stain—A differential stain used to identify bacteria that have mycolic acids in their cell wall.

AIDS (acquired immune deficiency syndrome)—The end stage of HIV infection characterized by opportunistic infections (infections caused by organisms that do not normally cause disease in a healthy human host). A patient with AIDS has a very low or nonexistent T lymphocyte count.

allergy—An excessive immune response to a foreign substance.

anergy—Lack of an immune response to a foreign substance.

antibiotic—An antimicrobial substance produced by another living organism or through manufacturing.

BCG vaccine—Bacille Calmette Guérin vaccine, originally formulated by Albert Calmette and Camille Guérin using *Mycobacterium bovis*. The vaccine protects against tuberculosis.

boosting—An enhanced immune response to tuberculin testing due to repeated testing.

bronchoscopy—A medical procedure in which a viewing instrument called a bronchoscope is inserted into the trachea to view the upper area of the lungs and take samples for lab analysis.

Calmette, Albert—Working at the Pasteur Institute at Lille, France, with Camille Guérin, he formulated the BCG vaccine.

caseous exudates—Thick secretions resulting from the decay of the tubercle due to the release of enzymes by bacteria and host cells.

catalase—An enzyme produced by many bacteria that detoxifies hydrogen peroxide by breaking it down into oxygen and water.

consumption—Antiquated term for tuberculosis.

cords—Filamentous aggregates of *Mycobacterium tuberculosis* observed when the organism grows in animal tissues.

cytokines—Hormonelike proteins produced by cells of the immune response, particularly lymphocytes and macrophages.

delayed hypersensitivity reaction—An exaggerated immune response involving T lymphocytes that manifests 48–72 hours after exposure to antigen.

directly observed therapy (DOT) — An effective therapy that relies on health-care workers to directly observe affected individuals taking their antitubercular medications.

droplet nuclei — Small liquid droplets containing bacteria. Often released during sneezing or deep coughing.

Galen — Greek physican who was interested in studying tuberculosis and systems of the human body. His prescription for tuberculosis included rest, diet, and fresh/salt air and was followed for almost 1,700 years.

genome — All of the genetic information contained in an organism.

giant cells — Large, multinucleated cells that result from the fusion of macrophages. Giant cells are one component of a tubercle.

granuloma — A lesion composed of macrophages, lymphocytes, bacteria, and host cells. The function of the granuloma is to wall off the infectious agent. In tuberculosis, a granuloma is called a tubercle.

Guérin, Camille — French veterinarian who, along with Albert Calmette, first produced the BCG vaccine.

hemoptysis — Coughing up blood from the respiratory tract.

HIV (human immunodeficiency virus) — A virus that infects T lymphocytes. The infection ultimately results in a depressed or absent immune response.

induration — A hard raised area on the skin.

inflammation — A host response to foreign substances or tissue damage. Inflammation is characterized by redness, heat, swelling, and pain in the area where it occurs.

Koch, Robert — German doctor and Nobel Prize winner who observed and identified *Mycobacterium tuberculosis* as the cause of tuberculosis in 1881.

Koch's postulates — A series of steps put forth by Robert Koch that are designed to identify the particular organism that causes a specific disease.

latent tuberculosis — A noninfectious and asymptomatic form of tuberculosis in which the bacteria are sequestered inside tubercles.

liquefaction — Process by which tissues become liquid due to the release of enzymes from cells.

lymphocytes — Cells that function in the specific immune response to eliminate foreign bodies or organisms. B lymphocytes produce antibodies, whereas T lymphocytes release cytokines or kill other cells.

lymphokines — Cytokines produced by lymphocytes.

lyse — To break open.

lysosome — A structure, particularly in macrophages, that contains digestive enzymes.

macrophage — A phagocytic cell that plays a major role in keeping the respiratory system free of microorganisms.

Mantoux, Charles — Formulated the Mantoux method of testing for tuberculosis which involves injecting tuberculin under the surface of the skin.

meerkat — Small, insect-eating mammals native to the dry regions of Africa.

miliary tuberculosis — A disseminated form of tuberculosis. The organism causes lesions to form in various parts of the body. The lesions resemble a grain called millet.

monocytes — White blood cells that will ultimately develop into macrophages.

multi-drug-resistant tuberculosis (MDR-TB) — Tuberculosis caused by tubercle bacilli that are resistant to two or more tuberculosis medications.

Mycobacterium bovis — Acid-fast bacilli most commonly found in cattle. The organism can cause tuberculosis in human beings.

Mycobacterium tuberculosis — A slender, rod-shaped, acid-fast bacterium that causes tuberculosis.

mycolic acid — Large, waxlike lipids that are found in the cell walls of acid-fast bacteria.

peptidoglycan — A major biochemical component of all bacterial cell walls.

phagolysosome — Structure that results from the fusion of the phagosome and the lysosome.

phagosome — A food storage vacuole inside a phagocytic cell.

phthisis — Antiquated term for tuberculosis.

Pott's disease — Tuberculosis of the spine.

purified protein derivative (PPD) — A form of tuberculin purified by Florence Seibert in 1934. PPD is used in the Mantoux test.

sanatorium—Special treatment facilities which housed tuberculosis patients. The sanatorium movement arose in the late 1890s and ended by the late 1950s.

scrofula—Tuberculosis of the lymph nodes.

Seibert, Florence—Researcher who purified tuberculin in 1934, producing a product called PPD.

sputum—Material coughed up from the lung.

streptomycin—Antibiotic isolated by Selman Waksman and his associates in 1943. Streptomycin was the first antibiotic used to successfully treat tuberculosis.

superoxide dismutase—An enzyme produced by bacteria, as well as other cells, and used to destroy toxic forms of oxygen.

T cell—See **lymphocyte.**

tine test—A tuberculosis test that uses a multipuncture device to deliver tuberculin just below the skin.

Trudeau, Edward—Founder of the Saranac Lake sanatorium. Dr. Trudeau was the first person in the United States to successfully culture the tubercle bacillus.

TU—Tuberculin units. Five TUs is the standard amount injected when performing a Mantoux tuberculin skin test.

tubercle—A granuloma produced as a result of *Mycobacterium tuberculosis* infection.

tuberculin—Heat-treated culture medium in which *Mycobacterium tuberculosis* was grown. Tuberculin may be used to screen patients for previous exposure to *Mycobacterium tuberculosis.*

virulence—An organism's ability to cause disease.

Waksman, Selman—The scientist who, along with his associates, discovered and purified streptomycin in 1943.

wheal—The pale, fluid-filled bubble that develops when tuberculin or PPD is injected under the skin.

Further Resources

BOOKS AND ARTICLES

Alcamo, I. Edward. *Fundamentals of Microbiology,* 5th ed. Menlo Park, Calif.: Benjamin Cummings, 1997.

Alexander, K. A., E. Pleydell, M. C. Williams, E. P. Lane, J. F. C. Nyange, and A. L. Michel. "*Mycobacterium tuberculosis*: An emerging disease of free-ranging wildlife." *Emerging Infectious Diseases* 8 (2002): 598–601.

American Thoracic Society. "Diagnostic Standards and Classification of Tuberculosis in Adults and Children." *American Journal of Respiratory and Critical Care Medicine* 161 (2000): 1376–1395.

Armus, Diego. *The Ailing City: Health, Tuberculosis, and Culture in Buenos Aires, 1870–1950.* Durham, N.C.: Duke University Press, 2011.

Berthet, F., M. Lagranderie, P. Gounon, C. Laurent-Winter, D. Ensergueix, P. Chavarot, D. Portnoi, G. Marchal, and B. Gicquel. "Attenuation of Virulence by Disruption of the *Mycobacterium tuberculosis erp* Gene." *Science* 282 (1998): 759–762.

Bloom, Barry R., ed. *Tuberculosis: Pathogenesis, Protection, and Control.* Washington, D.C.: ASM Press, 1994.

Bloom, Barry R., and Christopher J. L. Muray. "Tuberculosis: Commentary on a Reemergent Killer." *Science* 257 (1992): 1055–1061.

Centers for Disease Control and Prevention. "Development of New Vaccines for Tuberculosis." *Morbidity and Mortality Weekly Report.* 47 (1998): 1–6.

Centers for Disease Control and Prevention. "Targeted Tuberculin Testing and Treatment of Latent Tuberculosis Infection." *Morbidity and Mortality Weekly Report* 49 (2000): 1–53.

Charles, Frederick. *The Relation of Climate to the Treatment of Pulmonary Tuberculosis (1910).* Whitefish, Mont.: Kessinger Publishing, 2010.

Cole, S. T., R. Brosch, J. Parkhill, T. Garnier, C. Churcher, D. Harris et al. "Deciphering the biology of *Mycobacterium tuberculosis* from the complete genome sequence." *Nature* 393 (1998): 515–516.

Connolly, Cynthia. *Saving Sickly Children: The Tuberculosis Preventorium in American Life, 1909–1970.* Piscataway, N.J.: Rutgers University Press, 2008.

Cosivi, O., J. M. Grange, C. J. Daborn, M. C. Raviglioine, T. Fujikura, D. Cousins, R. A. Robinson, H. F. A. K. Huchzermeyer, I. de Kantor, and F. X. Meslin. "Zoonotic tuberculosis due to *Mycobacterium bovis* in developing countries." *Emerging Infectious Diseases* 4 (1998): 59–70.

Cowley, G., E. A. Leonard, and M. Hager. "A Deadly Return." *Newsweek,* March 16, 1992, 53–57.

Daniel, Thomas M. *Captain of Death: The Story of Tuberculosis.* Rochester, N.Y.: University of Rochester Press, 1997.

Dobell, Horace. *On the Nature, Cause and Treatment of Tuberculosis.* 1866. Reprint. Charleston, S.C.: BiblioBazaar, 2009.

Dormandy, Thomas. *The White Death: A History of Tuberculosis.* New York: New York University Press, 1999.

Dubnau, E., P. Fontan, R. Manganelli, S. Soares-Appel, and I. Smith. "*Mycobacterium tuberculosis* genes induced during infection of human macrophages." *Infection and Immunity* 70 (2002): 2787–2795.

Dubos, R., and J. Dubos. *The White Plague: Man and Society.* New Brunswick, N.J.: Rutgers University Press, 1987.

Dyer, Carol. *Tuberculosis.* Santa Barbara, Calif.: Greenwood Press, 2010.

Ezzell, Carol. "Captain of the Men of Death." *Science News* 143 (1993): 90–92.

"Focus on AIDS in New York State." Albany: New York State Department of Health. AIDS Institute (Spring 1993).

Kahn, E. A., and J. R. Starke. "Diagnosis of Tuberculosis in Children: Increased Need for Better Methods." *Emerging Infectious Diseases* 1 (1995): 1–10.

Krajick, Kevin. "Floating Zoo." *Discover* (February 1997): 67–73.

Laurence, Jeffrey. "TB and AIDS: An Issue of Extraordinary Importance." *The AIDS Reader* (September/October 1992): 147–178.

Lutwick, Larry I., ed. *Tuberculosis.* London: Chapman Hall Medical, 1995.

Mamunes, George. *So Has a Daisy Vanished: Emily Dickinson and Tuberculosis.* Jefferson, N.C.: McFarland and Co., 2007.

Mayho, Paul, Richard Coker, and Marcos Espinal. *The Tuberculosis Survival Handbook.* Boca Raton, Fla.: Merit Publishing International, 2010.

Michalak, K., C. Austin, S. Diesel, J. Maichle Bacon, P. Zimmerman, and J. N. Maslow. "*Mycobacterium tuberculosis* infection as a zoonotic disease: Transmission between humans and elephants." *Emerging Infectious Diseases* 4 (1998): 283–287.

Paris, Gloria. *A Child of Sanitariums: A Memoir of Tuberculosis Survival and Lifelong Disability.* Jefferson, N.C.: McFarland and Co., 2010.

Reichman, Lee B., and E. S. Hershfield, eds. *Tuberculosis.* 2d ed. New York: Marcel Dekker, 2000.

Reichman, Lee B., and Janice Hopkins Tanne. *Timebomb: The Global Epidemic of Multidrug Resistant Tuberculosis.* New York: McGraw Hill, 2002.

Roberts, Charlotte, and Jane Buikstra. *The Bioarcheology of Tuberculosis: A Global View on a Reemerging Disease.* Gainesville: University Press of Florida, 2008.

Rom, W. M., and S. Garay, eds. *Tuberculosis.* New York: Little, Brown, 1995.

Schlossberg, D., ed. *Tuberculosis and Nontuberculosis Mycobacterial Infections.* Philadelphia: W.B. Saunders, 1999.

Sompayrac, Lauren. *How the Immune System Works.* Malden, Mass.: Blackwell Science, 1999.

Sontag, Susan. *Illness as Metaphor.* Toronto: McGraw-Hill Ryerson, 1977.

Talaro, Kathleen P., and Arthur Talaro. *Foundations in Microbiology.* 4th ed. New York: McGraw-Hill, 2002.

Yancey, Diane. *Tuberculosis.* Minneapolis: Lerner Publishing Group, 2008.

Young, D. B., and B. D. Robertson. "TB Vaccines: Global Solutions for Global Problems." *Science* 284 (1999): 1479–1480.

WEB SITES

Adirondack Museum Tuberculosis Information
http://www.adirondackmuseum.net/ho/tb/tbkwrd.html

American Lung Association
http://www.lungusa.org

American Thoracic Society
http://www.thoracic.org

Brown University TB/HIV Research Laboratory
http://www.brown.edu/Research/TB-HIV_Lab

Centers for Disease Control and Prevention
http://www.cdc.gov

Charles P. Felton National Tuberculosis Center
http://www.harlemtbcenter.org

eMedicinehealth
http://www.emedicinehealth.com/tuberculosis/article_em.htm

Francis J. Curry National Tuberculosis Center
http://www.nationaltbcenter.edu

Mayo Clinic
http://www.mayoclinic.com/health/tuberculosis/DS00372

MedicineNet.com
http://www.medicinenet.com/tuberculosis/article.htm

National Library of Medicine
http://www.nlm.nih.gov/medlineplus/tuberculosis.html

New Jersey Medical School National Tuberculosis Center
http://www.umdnj.edu/ntbcweb/newbldg.htm

STOP TB Homepage
http://www.stoptb.org/world.tb.day/WTBD_2002/default.asp#Background

TIGR, *Mycobacterium tuberculosis* Genome
http://www.tigr.org/tigr-scripts/CMR2/GenomePage3.spl?database=gmt

The Trudeau Institute
http://www.trudeauinstitute.org/

Tuberculosis, Ancient Enemy, Present Threat, National Institute of Allergies and Infectious Diseases
http://www.niaid.nih.gov/newsroom/focuson/tb02/tb.htm

Tuberculosis Fact Sheet, National Institute of Allergies and Infectious Diseases
http://www.niaid.nih.gov/factsheets/tb.htm

Tuberculosis Net, the Source for Tuberculosis Teaching Materials
http://tuberculosis.net

Tuberculosis Research Center, India
http://www.trc-chennai.org

Tuberculosis Resources, New York City Department of Health
http://www.cpmc.columbia.edu/tbcpp

World Health Organization Global TB Program
http://www.who.int/gtb

125

Kim R. Finer received her B.A. in microbiology at Miami University and her Ph.D. in veterinary microbiology at Texas A&M University. She is currently an associate professor in the Department of Biological Sciences at Kent State University, where she teaches courses in microbiology, human genetics, and ecology. She has written textbooks on the use of Internet resources in the classroom and has published numerous papers in the areas of biology education as well as in her research area. She received the Exxon Foundation Innovation in Education Award in 1996 and was elected to Who's Who Among America's Teachers in 1998. Dr. Finer was also recently identified as a national model course developer by the SENCER program of the Association of American Colleges and Universities. She lives in Wooster, Ohio, with her two teenage children, Ben and Julia, her husband John, and dog Jenny.

Dr. Alan I. Hecht is a practicing chiropractor in New York. He is also an adjunct professor at Farmingdale State College and Nassau Community College and an adjunct associate professor at the C.W. Post campus of Long Island University. He teaches courses in medical microbiology, health and human disease, anatomy and physiology, comparative anatomy, human physiology, embryology, and general biology. In addition he is the course coordinator for human biology at Hofstra University, where he is an adjunct assistant professor.

Dr. Hecht received his B.S. in biology–premedical studies from Fairleigh Dickinson University in Teaneck, New Jersey. He received his M.S. in basic medical sciences from New York University School of Medicine. He received his doctor of chiropractic (D.C.) degree from New York Chiropractic College in Brookville, New York.

About the Consulting Editor

Hilary Babcock, M.D., M.P.H., is an assistant professor of medicine at Washington University School of Medicine and the medical director of occupational health for Barnes-Jewish Hospital and St. Louis Children's Hospital. She received her undergraduate degree from Brown University and her M.D. from the University of Texas Southwestern Medical Center at Dallas. After completing her residency, chief residency, and infectious disease fellowship at Barnes-Jewish Hospital, she joined the faculty of the infectious disease division. She completed an M.P.H. in public health from St. Louis University School of Public Health in 2006. She has lectured, taught, and written extensively about infectious diseases, their treatment, and their prevention. She is a member of numerous medical associations and is board certified in infectious disease. She lives in St. Louis, Missouri.